C000153037

Planning the Liturgy with the Celebration Hymnal

Contents

INTRODUCTION

The main use of the Celebration Hymnal is to provide music for Mass. Sunday by Sunday someone – perhaps you – has to sit down and choose the words and music which will allow the people of God, whom you serve, to express their praise, their sorrow, and their prayer.

This is a task of great importance, because the Mass is no ordinary gathering. When the Christian people in your parish come together on Sunday, the Lord's Day, they are obeying Jesus's own command. He is really present among them and, as an old prayer still used in the Missal says:

> Each time we offer this memorial sacrifice
> the work of our redemption is accomplished.

(Prayer over the gifts, Maundy Thursday evening)

The parish musicians are privileged to have a part in this. What they do is a *ministry* – a service to the whole community.

The **Celebration Hymnal** contains 835 hymns and songs, and the thought of searching through all those each week is rather daunting. To make a good choice for a particular Sunday you need a guide to direct you to the most appropriate hymns, and that is the first purpose of this book.

Its secondary purpose is to give you, as someone concerned in music for the liturgy, a chance to think a little about what you do. Since you are reading this book, you are probably convinced that singing at Mass is a good thing. Some people in your congregation may need more convincing, although they will respond to the right kind of leadership (of which more is said in section 5 below.) To help you in your task, which is not always an easy one, some introductory chapters have been provided which deal with basic questions of liturgy, with the significance of singing and with what should be sung.

Choosing music for worship is not just a question of looking for your (or someone else's) favourite hymn. Worship is not the same as entertainment, it is the meeting of God and his people. The first question to ask of any song is not 'Do I like it?' but 'Does it serve its intended purpose in the liturgy?' To answer this, we have to know what that purpose might be.[1]

In fact, liturgical music has more than one purpose. Everything we use in the liturgy is more than it seems to be on the surface: water used

[1] The following paragraphs depend heavily on **Learning to Celebrate** by Fr Joseph Gelineau (Pastoral Press 1985), pp 47–51

in the liturgy is not *just* water, bread is not *just* bread. And so it is with music.

Music, first, has a human function. It creates certain moods: it is rousing, it is moving, it makes us happy or sad – this is the level at which we usually speak about music. It is also a means of expression, and a means of making a crowd of people into a united body. We wouldn't be human without music, even if nowadays we are usually (except, we hope, in the liturgy) passive consumers of it rather than performers. It is because music is so much a part of being human that it is of such use in the liturgy. Second, liturgical music has a *ritual* function. The Mass is a rite which, although its basic meaning and gestures originate from the Lord's command, has evolved over centuries. It contains a variety of ways of 'speaking'. There are proclamation, praise, and meditation; some pieces are sung by one person, some by everybody. Each piece of music in the mass has to be of the right form to fulfil its purpose. Music, in addition, is not the only kind of sound in the Mass; there is also speech and, very important, silence.

But beyond these two is a level which is special to music in worship: the *symbolic* function. This is when one asks not 'did the people enjoy it?' or 'was it all liturgically correct?' but 'was this a meeting of God and his people?' Music points to the beyond. It is only a signpost, not the destination. It can turn us to face the right direction, but also show us our limitations, for no matter how beautiful we make it, our music is only ever a pale reflection of God. It will always leave us yearning for something more, which is the vision of God when we hope to be 'lost in wonder, love and praise.'

Part One: What is the Liturgy?

1. MUSIC IN THE MASS

1a. What sort of music?

ALTHOUGH this is a book about a hymn-book, the first thing to emphasise is that there is more to music at Mass than hymns.

Hymns and songs as we know them today have only been regularly used at Mass since the late 1960s. Before that, the Mass was always in Latin and the choir sang chants taken from the Psalms.

When it became necessary to find music for the mass in English, people turned to existing hymns and hymnbooks, and since then new ones in various styles have been added to the repertoire. Many have proved very service-able. But the older hymns were not actually written for Mass at all, and newer ones follow the same pattern, so we have to ask: how do they fit in? Each part of the Mass, as the Introduction said, has a definite purpose, and whatever is sung must serve it. We have to fit music to the Mass, not the other way round.

Word and Eucharist
Worship is a meeting between God and the people he has created. It is God who takes the first step. He brings us together, he speaks to us, he nourishes us. We listen and take his Word to heart; and to show that we have received it, we respond in thanksgiving. We then go out, filled with the life of God, to do His bidding.

God makes his presence known to us in many ways, but two are of special interest to us here because they have shaped our worship; they are Word and Eucharist. The two main parts of the Mass are the **Liturgy of the Word** (from the First Reading to the Bidding Prayer) and the **Liturgy of the Eucharist** (from the Preparation of the Gifts – the old Offertory – to the Prayer after Communion). These are the vital parts of the Mass, but not all of it: it begins with an Entrance or 'gathering' rite,

and ends with a Concluding Rite but these, although they take up time and attention, are not of such vital importance.

Word
The Liturgy of the Word is the most variable part of the Mass. The story of the great things God has done for us cannot be absorbed all at once. It is proclaimed in a thousand different ways in the course of the year and even then we only take in a fraction of it. It is a lifetime's work to ponder on the Word of God and try to discern its message.

Hymns and songs are an extension of the Word – they provide us with ways of expressing the truths that we have heard, in our own fashion. This is why it is so important to choose the right hymns for the Sunday or season. One of the Scripture passages is itself a song, the Responsorial Psalm, which, because it is part of the Word of God, should not be replaced by any old hymn. The Gospel Acclamation is usually taken from Scripture as well.

From Word to Thanksgiving
The Mass is an 'exchange of vows', rather as in marriage. To put it as the bible would, it is a Covenant. God speaks his Word of love and we receive and acknowledge it. This exchange is then sealed by a sacramental act in which the promise is given bodily form – the Eucharist (Greek for 'thanksgiving').

Eucharist In the Word we hear of God's great works for his people. In the Eucharist he actually performs them among us again.

The Liturgy of the Eucharist is less variable than the Liturgy of the Word, although in the first section of the Eucharistic Prayer, the Preface, we have a wonderful variety of texts. The actions of the Liturgy of the Eucharist are still essentially those which Jesus commanded us, at the Last Supper, to 'do in memory' of him: he *took* bread, *blessed* it, *broke* it, and *gave* it to his disciples; and likewise with the cup. These actions are still seen in the Preparation of Gifts, the Eucharistic Prayer, the Breaking of Bread and the Communion.

From Thanksgiving to Doing
The covenant act of God and his people in the Eucharist is called the 'source and summit' of the Christian life. The summit, because it is the most sacred part of the Church's activity, and the source, because it gives us the strength to take Christ to the world until we gather once again.

The Shape of the Mass and Music
It is important to get used to the Word/Eucharist shape of the Mass so that it comes as second nature.

Music can help us to do this. Singing at the key points of the Mass will indicate their meaning and importance and help us to take part with understanding.

The following paragraphs attempt to say what these key points are, and they are summarised in the chart on p.16. This chart, which puts the sung parts of the Mass in order of importance, is based on *Music for the Mass,* a chart published by the Bishops' Committee on Church Music, 1987, and its debt to this latter is hereby acknowledged. This chart may be open to criticism in details, but overall it is a faithful reflection of what is said in the most official teaching we have about the Mass, the *General Instruction on the Roman Missal - (GIRM)*.

One word of caution. When reading these pages and the chart it is important to avoid the 'musician's-eye view' of the Mass, which sees it as a series of isolated musical highlights (done by musicians) surrounded by a hazy sea of words. This is as ridiculous as the view from the other end (not unknown among Catholics) of the Mass as a time for quiet prayer which is punctuated by unwanted intrusions from musicians!

Music shouldn't be thought of as an extra, or an irrelevance, but as *part of the rite itself*, as carols are a part of Christmas. If you feel that a Mass without music is somehow incomplete, you know what is meant. But don't look at the music in isolation; you cannot take part intelligently in the music if you don't take part in the whole action. Each sung part only has full meaning when seen in relation to everything else.

Acclamations The most important moments of the Mass are the Gospel and the Eucharistic Prayer. Naturally these are emphasised by music; respectively, the Gospel Acclamation (Alleluia or its Lenten equivalent) and the Acclamations of the Eucharistic Prayer (three at present: Holy, holy, Memorial Acclamation and Amen.) There is a selection of Eucharistic Liturgies in the front of the Celebration Hymnal, and Gospel Acclamations are to be found in *The Responsorial Psalter* and similar books, although there is a small selection in the Celebration Hymnal (e.g. 685, 697 and 698); there are also some 'Alleluia songs' such as 377, 424, 494 or 593 which could be used as Gospel acclamations, e.g. at Christmas (377) or Easter (424, 494). No 788 is a Lenten Gospel Acclamation. If some of these seem longer than your usual acclamation, remember that the Alleluia is really a *processional* song and so can be extended to accompany the movement of the Gospel book (if the Church has one) to its place of honour at the lectern. Nos 697 and 698 lend themselves well to this treatment as they can be extended indefinitely.

At the other end of the scale, you can sing a very simple alleluia. If the music at Mass (even on a weekday) consisted simply of singing a Gospel Acclamation and a Holy, Holy it would be a good start. And it's not impossible. You don't even need books and instruments; people can learn short pieces off by heart and sing unaccompanied if they are motivated enough.

Because of their importance, the Gospel Acclamation and the Eucharistic Acclamations are put in the first column in the chart.

Songs of the Rite Two other parts of the Mass which are songs, and which logically should be sung rather than recited, are the **Glory to God** and the **Responsorial Psalm.**

There are five settings of the Gloria in the

Eucharist section of the hymnbook. The Psalm is not so easy to cater for in the space available to the Celebration Hymnal. Sometimes the text of the psalm of the day can be found among nos. 665–692, the psalm section, and where this happens it is noted in the Sunday lists. Some hymns are based on the psalms, and Taizé chants sometimes have psalm verses and correspond with the Sunday psalm; these are listed in the index. But if you want to sing the text of the Lectionary every week you will need the Responsorial Psalter or equivalent.

Hymns Hymns haven't been mentioned at all yet! This is a way of making the point that it is important to make sure that the *actual texts* of the liturgy, i.e. what you find in the Missal and

Lectionary, are sung. This may not be the experience in every parish. For many people, music at mass just means *hymns*. If this is so, there is something missing. The reason why the chart puts the four hymns that we usually sing (Entrance, Preparation of Gifts, Communion and Recessional) in only the third column is not because they are of little importance, but because in a well-prepared liturgy they should *not* be sung without the parts mentioned above. If they are, you get the famous 'hymn sandwich', when everything is sung *except* what is in the Missal, surely not what was intended.

Let us assume though that yours is a well-balanced liturgy, though, and examine these songs in turn.

The Introductory Rites and the Entrance Song

The purpose of the Entrance Song is, according to the *General Instruction*, to *open the celebration, intensify the union of the gathered people, lead their thoughts to the mystery of the season or feast, and accompany the procession of priest and ministers (25)*.

To choose an entrance song, you could either go to the list of hymns for the Sunday or to the Entrance section of the general Index. In one of the big seasons such as Lent, Eastertide or Advent, it is not too difficult to find a seasonal hymn. On Sundays in Ordinary Time it may not be so easy, and this is where the index is useful. One basic idea for an Entrance song is *gathering,* and in fact the term Gathering Song is another name for it. Gathering for the Sunday celebration of the Resurrection, coming into the presence of the Lord, are expressed in hymns such as *Again the Lord's own day is here* (386), *We are gathering together unto him* (341), *What is this place?* (818) and many others, such as versions of Psalm 94(95) or 99(100).

If you want an extended period of gathering, even starting well before the time Mass is due to begin, Taizé chants are designed for such purposes (at Pentecost, no 638, *Veni Sancte*

Spiritus, is another example). Some of them could even be extended into a Pentitential Rite, e.g. *Ostende nobis* (711) in Advent.

Repeating an Entrance Song several Sundays running, particularly during an important season, is a way of uniting the season and learning new music. This works best if you have a cantor or choir, so that you can use songs with a chorus to be repeated by solo or choir verses. Here are some examples – you can search for others:

   16 A voice cries (Advent)
  391 All you nations (General)
  430 Christ our Lord has come (Easter)
  431 Christ our Pasch (Easter)
  435 Come, let us ring out our joy (General)
  436 Come, Lord Jesus (Advent)
  640 Wake up! the time is near (Advent)
  711 Ostende nobis (Advent)
  728 Bless the Lord, my soul (Lent)
  733 Come to set us free (Advent)
  739 Father, we come to you (General)
  748 God, your glory we have seen (Easter)
  751 Hear us, Almighty Lord (Lent)
  789 Prepare ye the way (Advent)
  805 Wait for the Lord (Advent)

Repetition need not be boredom; in fact, the more familiar people are with a piece the more likely they are to enjoy singing it. Singing a hymn (or Mass setting) several weeks running is a technique which can be used for any new music until it is learnt.

When choosing an Entrance/ Gathering song, remember that it may be followed by a Penitential Rite *and* Gloria, so it can be some time before you reach the Liturgy of the Word. You have to decide whether you really need to sing all three items. When the Gloria is not sung, in Lent or Advent, the Penitential Rite can be extended or integrated with the Entrance Hymn. No 780, *O Lord be not mindful*, forms a Penitential Rite in itself and

711, mentioned above, could be used both as Gathering Song and Penitential Rite. In the Eucharist Section, Penitential Rites I and II can be extended as desired by putting in invocations either from the Missal or specially composed.

In Eastertide, by contrast, the penitential rite can be given less prominence and the Gloria more. And as this is a Baptismal season, it is an appropriate time to use the alternative to the Penitential Rite, the **Rite of Blessing of Water.** There is a song tailor-made for this, *Water of Life*, the first piece in the book. (Nos 430 *Christ the Lord has come to save his people* or 621 *There is one Lord* could also be used, and 757 *In the abundance of your compassion* serves the same function in Lent.)

Liturgy of the Word

The Introductory Rites end with the opening prayer, as the chart shows. The music for the Liturgy of the Word, as explained above, is mainly to be found in a cantor's book such as the *Responsorial Psalter*. It was also explained that in the Liturgy of the Word the musician's task is to *listen and respond* with everyone else as God speaks and 'these words are being fulfilled today, even as you listen' (Luke 4:21, Sunday 3/C). Unless we give the Word our full

attention how can we then 'speak' as musicians?

The readings are followed by the Homily, Profession of Faith and Intercessions, in which the 'priestly people' prays to God for the needs of the Church, the world and the local community. To give power to the Intercessions, use a sung response; see the Divine Office section (words edition pp.345 or 350), or no 710.

Liturgy of the Eucharist

The Preparation of the Gifts
Although most people still talk of the 'Offertory', the name was changed twenty years ago to 'Preparation of the Gifts', because the old prayers of offering were removed and the present ones put in their place. The real 'offering' of the Mass takes place not now but in the Eucharistic Prayer.

The key word is *Preparation*. This is a moment in which while the gifts and altar are prepared, people can pause for thought before embarking on the great prayer of thanksgiv-

ing. It shouldn't be overloaded with music or ritual.

It is a suitable place for choir or singing group to sing, perhaps taking one of the less familiar pieces in the book and elaborating on it. Besides allowing scope for musical talent, which after all is there for a purpose, it is a way of teaching new music, because you can ask people to join in with the same song next week.

The second section of the Liturgy of the Eucharist is the **Eucharistic Prayer.** The hymnbook contains six Eucharistic Liturgies (by which is meant sets of acclamations – Holy holy, memorial acclamation, amen) and a seventh set included in the *New People's Mass* (see more on this below, section Ib). Once again, the musicians' task is to take part in the prayer fully, with heart and voice, in company with the whole assembly (and the angels in heaven, as the Preface says!) and not worry about the next piece of music.

The Communion Rite

The Communion Rite is the third part of the Liturgy of the Eucharist. In order to put us in the right frame of mind for receiving the Bread of Life and the Cup of Blessing, there are some rites of preparation:

In the **Our Father** we pray for our daily bread (by which we also mean the bread of the eucharist),

In the **Rite of Peace** we show that we have no quarrel with our fellow-worshippers, which would make us unworthy to go to the Lord's table.

After this comes the **Breaking of Bread.** This is a simple gesture – Jesus broke a loaf to give a piece to each disciple. Over the centuries (since the Acts of the Apostles where we find the Eucharist called 'the Breaking of Bread' (2:42 and elsewhere)) it has acquired a deeper meaning, and the *General Instruction* (56c) says: *We, though many in number, become one body because we eat the one bread of Life which is Christ.* It has its own music to accompany it, the **Lamb of God,** introduced into the Mass in the 8th century for this purpose. It is in litany form, and so it may be extended beyond the usual three-fold version. It will need to be extended if there are many hosts to be broken and the action of breaking takes longer than usual. For this reason three settings of the Lamb of God given in the Eucharist section have extra verses and can be extended to cover not only the Breaking of Bread but the Communion as well.

What we usually think of as the **Communion Song** is the song which accompanies the communion procession, about which the *General Instruction* (56i) says *Its purpose is to express the spiritual union of the communicants by the union of the voices, to show forth their joy, and to make it clear that the Communion Procession is a fraternal occasion.* It is quite an important song, therefore.

But is this importance apparent in practice? Experience shows that this is the least successful of the songs of the Mass. It is inconvenient to take a book up to communion with you, and few people want to start singing immediately they come back to their place. Many people simply feel that singing at communion is inappropriate. To translate the vision of the GIRM into reality is, therefore, faced with serious problems. There would seem to be three solutions, listed here from the worst case to the ideal. You could:

– put off the singing until after communion (easy way out)
– leave the choir to sing or the instrumentalists to play on their own
– invite the people to sing an easily memorised refrain (such as a Taizé chant or a psalm response) while cantor or choir sing the verses. Here are some examples:

380	A new commandment
403	As one body
526	Keep in mind
671	My soul is thirsting for the Lord
683	I will walk in the presence of the Lord
696	Adoramus te, Domine
728	Bless the Lord, my soul
778	O Christe Domine Jesu
822	Unless a grain of wheat

The singing may even start *before* communion. In the Eucharist section there are three extendable settings of the **Lamb of God,** nos 2–4. These are designed to be used not just to accompany the Breaking of Bread (the original function of the Lamb of God) but, by exploiting the litany form by including extra invocations (you can add more of your own), to provide a song for the Communion Procession as well. As the music will have been already established before Communion, it will not be such a problem to sustain it during the procession. Thus this part of the Mass will be given a unity which it should have but which it sometimes lacks.

It may not be easy to get singing at

Communion started on an ordinary Sunday, when people are not so receptive to new ideas! There is more chance of it happening when, for instance, there is a long communion procession such as at Christmas, Good Friday or Easter, or some special occasion such as the parish confirmation, a Day of Recollection, or a young people's Mass, when people are more open than usual to participating in different ways. Once the Communion Song has been established as a possibility, you have got over one hurdle.

The **Communion Thanksgiving Song** (the first choice mentioned above) is something else to be considered. The *General Instruction* (56j) has this to say: '*After communion, the priest and people may spend some time in silent prayer. If desired, a hymn, psalm or other song of praise may be sung by the entire congregation.*' Singing at this point is greatly effective. Unlike many of the songs of the Mass the Communion Thanksgiving song is sung for its own sake, when nothing else is happening; it can thus be given people's full attention. It also ensures that, even if there was no singing during the actual procession, communion does not go by devoid of all musical expression.

Because it comes so near to the end of Mass, though, it is usually dropped in favour of a Recessional Hymn. But there is a good case for singing a hymn here rather than at the end of Mass. In the body of the Planner you will frequently find the abbreviation CT/R (Communion Thanksgiving/Recessional) suggesting that the sort of hymn usually sung at the end might be better after Communion.

The Concluding Rite and the Final Song

The Concluding Rite comprises the prayer after Communion, the blessing and the dismissal. The Final Song is not mentioned at all in the General Instruction on the Roman Missal but almost invariably one is sung. However, since the last words addressed to the people are 'Go in peace to love and serve the Lord', it could be argued that this is the right moment to finish the celebration, so that mission takes up where worship leaves off.

However, there are some good songs written with this moment in mind, such as 'Forth in the peace of Christ we go' (78; see also the new version, no 744.) If you use rounds or Taizé chants, you can have an extended concluding song which people can sing even while processing out of church; for instance *Surrexit Christus* (796), *Go out to the whole world* (703), *Jubilate Deo* (706). The singing can be extended *ad libitum* until there is a general consensus that it should stop!

Even if you sing a recessional hymn regularly, it could be omitted on some days of the year, such as Palm Sunday, Good Friday and maybe some Sundays in Lent, to point out the special character of these days.

1b. Using the Eucharist Section

For Catholics the most frequent act of worship is the Mass. This Introduction has already said more than once that hymns and songs are not the only music in the Mass, so that these days a hymnbook, to be practical, needs something more. This is why the *Celebration Hymnal* has an extensive section of 'Mass chants'.

This section cannot claim to be comprehensive and satisfy the needs of every parish. You will probably have favourite Mass settings in your parish already, and continue to use them. What it does aim to do, though, is:

1. to show by the way it is arranged that each part of a 'mass setting' serves a different

function in the Mass. For example, the Gloria is a hymn of praise which the missal calls 'a rite in itself', i.e. it does not accompany an action, whereas the Lamb of God is a litany which is intended to be sung during the Breaking of Bread. Apart, therefore, from the *New People's Mass*, which has been left together for ease of reference, the pieces in this section have been grouped by liturgical categories.

2. to make the point that you don't have to choose everything for one celebration from the same setting. Most of the Eucharistic Liturgies in this selection were in fact written as independent pieces and not as part of a whole Mass.

What to learn first It has already been said that the Acclamations of the Eucharistic Prayer are among the most important parts of the Mass for singing purposes. Every parish should have a *Holy holy,* one or other of the *Memorial acclamations* and a *Great Amen* which everyone knows and which can be sung with ease on big occasions such as Christmas and Easter.

Why is so much stress put on this?

Because the Eucharistic Prayer is, as the Missal says, *the centre and high point of the entire celebration (GIRM 57).*

We need to remind ourselves of this from time to time; since at this point we (usually) kneel down and listen, we are all tempted to relax and let our minds drift off. We have to acquire the habit of *consciously praying* the whole prayer. It is our prayer as well as the priest's, even though he actually utters most of the words and has the power of consecration. In the words of the GIRM: *The meaning of the prayer is that the whole congregation joins Christ in acknowledging the works of God and in offering the sacrifice.*(57)

If we are praying the prayer together with the priest, it will be easier to join in the sung parts and use them as our opportunity to show that we are all of one mind. A simple scheme of a typical Eucharistic Prayer will help to put them in context. Eucharistic Prayers all contain the same basic elements, although not always in quite the same order:

1. Dialogue (The Lord be with you, etc)
2. The Preface (a prayer of thanksgiving), ending in **Sanctus (Holy, holy).**
3. Continuation of the thanksgiving ('post-Sanctus') dwelling on the life and work of Jesus
4. Invocation of the Holy Spirit upon the gifts
5. 'Institution narrative' and Consecration, followed by the **Memorial acclamation (Christ has died..)**
6. a section 'remembering' the passion, death, resurrection, ascension and coming in glory of the Lord; known by the Greek word for remembering, *anamnesis.*
7. Intercessions (for the living and for the dead)
8. Doxology and **Great Amen.**

The liturgy is always developing, and it may be that, as in the Eucharistic Prayers for Children, more congregational acclamations will be added to the three we have normally. In the meantime, let us at least get those three sung!

Where do you start? As said above, a parish should have at least *one* set of acclamations that everyone knows. The Eucharistic Liturgies in this book are of varying levels of difficulty, although they are all within a normal congregation's capacity to learn. Start with a simple one and, to make sure that it is learnt properly, use it for several weeks in succession (It is not so boring as musicians might think to repeat the same music week after week; singing goes much better if people feel at ease and can join in something they know.)

Of the settings in the Eucharist section, no.5 is probably the easiest. It was written with folk groups in mind. No 1 (Farrell) is not difficult and allows for elaboration. Nos 3 and 6 are also 'general purpose' and no 2, the Celtic Liturgy, should prove popular although it needs a little more effort to get hold of and must be sung with feeling. No 4, the Coventry music, is more festive and would serve for a big occasion.

How do you teach the congregation new music? This is a perennial question.

15

Something more is said about this in section 5; but basically you have only two options: teaching people directly (i.e., 'Now we are going to learn some new music'; or indirectly: 'The choir are going to sing/the organist is going to play a new hymn which I would like you to listen to...) Most often, the second method is used, but the instruction is omitted and the people, although they are expected to join in, have to guess what is happening, which is bad manners on the part of the musicians and doesn't help people to become enthusiastic about singing.

In the case of something as important as Mass chants, the direct method might be used. Even with direct teaching, though, the music may not be picked up first time, but this is not a fatal blow; you should think in terms of months – even a year – for something to get established, if you are convinced that it is worth it. Don't try to learn a whole set of acclamations (e.g. the Celtic Liturgy) on the same day, but introduce them over a period of time. And to repeat, it is a good idea to use new Eucharist music several weeks running when it is first being learnt.

Music for the Mass

		1	2	3	4	5
Opening Rites:	Entrance/Gathering Song			•		
	Greeting					•
	Penitential Rite				•	
	Gloria		•			
	Opening Prayer					•
LITURGY OF THE WORD	*First Reading*					
	Responsorial Psalm		•			
	Second Reading					
	GOSPEL ACCLAMATION	•				
	GOSPEL					
	Homily					
	Profession of Faith					•
	Prayer of the Faithful				•	
LITURGY OF THE EUCHARIST Preparation of the Gifts:	Procession of Gifts					
	Song at the Procession			•		
Eucharistic Prayer:	Preface Dialogue and Preface				•	
	HOLY, HOLY	•			•	
	First part of prayer				•	
	MEMORIAL ACCLAMATION	•			•	
	Second part of prayer				•	
	AMEN	•			•	
Communion Rite:	Our Father				•	
	Sign of Peace					
	Breaking of Bread					
	Lamb of God				•	
	Communion Song			•		
	Communion Thanksgiving Song			•		
Concluding Rite	*Prayer after Communion*					
	Blessing					•
	Final Song			•		

2. THE SEASONS OF THE YEAR

Planning the music for a single Mass is one dimension of liturgical preparation. Planning for a whole season is another.

The Paschal Triduum

Start with what is most important. Just as the Christian week has a centre – Sunday – so does the Christian year. The centre of the Christian year is the 'Paschal Triduum', the three last days of Holy Week. In these days the passion, death and resurrection of Christ are celebrated and made present in the most solemn way. Appropriately, the Easter Vigil is the principal time of the year for Baptism, which is a dying and rising to new life with Christ.

Lent/Eastertide

Lent, or the **Forty Days,** is a time of preparation for baptism, or for the renewal of baptismal vows for those already baptised. It is for this reason that it is a penitential season, but the spirit of this penitence is in the words of the Gospel 'Repent and believe the Good News!' or in the words of the hymn, *Attend and keep this happy fast* (25). During Lent there occur the important rites of Initiation (RCIA), when after a long time of preparation those preparing for baptism suddenly see their goal in view, and there is a series of celebrations as part of the preparation: the Rite of Election in the Cathedral at the beginning of Lent and the Scrutinies on the 3rd, 4th and 5th Sundays, which take place at the parish Sunday Mass.

After the Paschal Triduum comes the Fifty Days, i.e. *Eastertide*, of which the Roman Calendar says: 'The fifty days from Easter Sunday to Pentecost are celebrated as one feast day, sometimes called "the great Sunday." The happiest people will be the newly baptised and this period is known for them as the time of *Mystagogia*, or, in plain English, of further teaching about the mysteries they have just celebrated. If we feel the temptation to go flat after the excitement of Holy Week and Easter Sunday, we should counteract this in every way we can. The Church wants the whole season to be a joyful one. A special Gloria and Alleluia, and the use of the Water rite before Sunday Mass instead of the Penitential Rite, are recommended.

The 40 days, 3 days and 50 days together form the Lent-Easter cycle which is the most important of the year.

Advent/Christmas

The other great season is of course the **Advent-Christmas** cycle, and this goes from the First Sunday of Advent to the feast of the Baptism of the Lord, which is the Sunday after the Epiphany. In purely human terms this is the season that people like best, and Easter still suffers by comparison; but the eyes of faith should tell us that it was the Resurrection which brought our salvation and Easter must be the centre of the year.

Looking at the readings for the Advent-Christmas cycle, it is striking to see the similarity between its beginning and its end. The readings for the Baptism of the Lord, which makes the end of Christmastide, echo or even repeat passages which have already been used in Advent. Though Christmas is the children's feast, adult Christians must search for meanings in it as well and the liturgy presents several: the light of Christ, the Word made flesh, the *mission* of Jesus (see a hymn such as Hail to the Lord's anointed, 110) and the coming of Jesus not just to Israel but to the whole world (All the ends of the earth, 724).

Ordinary Time

The rest of the year is known rather prosaically as **Ordinary Time** although the new Lectionary introduced as a result of the Vatican II reforms has made it potentially a time for receiving great spiritual riches. The opening up of the Scriptures which the Council asked for has borne abundant fruit in the provision of the three cycles of Sunday Gospel readings, with the Old Testament readings and psalms chosen to fit them. Listening to the different ways in which the evangelists write about Jesus (Matthew in Year A, Mark in Year B and Luke in year C) will, when we have experienced several cycles, greatly enrich our knowledge and love of our Lord. (There is a weak, or debatable point about the readings in Ordinary Time, in that the Second Readings (from a New Testament epistle) are not chosen to harmonise with the rest of the liturgy of the word, but form their own separate cycle.)

In the body of this Planner there is an introduction to each cycle which points out a few of the characteristics of each evangelist.

3. MUSIC IN THE DIVINE OFFICE

The Divine Office, otherwise called the Liturgy of the Hours or the Prayer of the Church, is a vital part of the church's life which has suffered from severe neglect for a very long time. What is it, and why *has* it been neglected?

We are all used to the idea of saying morning and night prayers, and perhaps the Angelus at midday and 6pm, thus marking out the times of the day with prayer. Most likely we would think of this as *private* prayer, but there are still even now places in the world where ordinary Christians come together several times a day to pray in common. In our part of the world, this only happens in monasteries and convents, and so we think of the Office as something priests and nuns do, but not lay people.

The idea of common prayer at set times each day is a very old one. It was already established in Jewish life before the time of Jesus, and right at the start of the Christian church we see signs of it in Acts (e.g. 4:24).

Over the course of the centuries these times of prayer developed into the Office. But something unfortunate happened as well: the people stopped coming to celebrate it, leaving the clergy and religious orders praying on their own. So it came to seem as though the Office was not the laity's business at all. It was still the official prayer of the Church; but the participation of the laity in it, as in many aspects of the Church's life, was not thought of as important.

In our own day, when so many Christian traditions are being rediscovered, the Church has said clearly and unmistakably:

The public and communal prayer of the people of God is truly one of the primary responsibilities of the Church (*General Instruction on the Liturgy of the Hours, 1.*)

It may take a while before the truth of this statement becomes clear. We have had to get used to a lot of new ways of thinking and acting and this may seem like one more chore. But there is still a great thirst for prayer in the Church, and this, coupled with the way we have learned to celebrate the liturgy actively and communally, makes now a good time to direct people's desire to pray into the traditional channels, giving back to everybody the common forms of prayer evolved by the Church over the centuries.

The Office is:

1. Prayer at set times of day (and night), related to the rhythms of nature (light and darkness) and human life (getting up, working, going to bed.)
2. Prayer which ideally should be communal and sung.
3. A prayer of praise and supplication. The old expression 'sacrifice of praise' expresses it; 'sacrifice' in the sense of something dedicated to God, made holy. It is the making holy of the whole day.
4. A prayer which is offered up unceasingly by the Church, the body of Christ, so that St Paul's words 'Pray without ceasing' (I Thess 5:17) are made reality.

Celebrating the Office

Where do you start?

It's one thing to make big recommendations, and another to translate them into action. The Office is unfamiliar territory compared with, say, the Mass. However, it is not as complicated as all that. The individual Hours all contain:

- a hymn;

- a psalm or psalms;
- a reading;
- prayers.

The Hours in the present arrangement are:

Morning prayer

Prayer during the day (before, at, or after midday)

Evening prayer

Night prayer

- and the **Office of Readings,** which can be at any time of day.

Morning and Evening Prayer were called the 'pivots of the Office' by Vatican II and so are the most important Hours. The Celebration Hymnal concentrates its attention principally on these two hours but Night Prayer (Compline) is also included.

There are two ways in which you could sing Morning or Evening Prayer in your parish or community: as it is in the official books, or by adapting it to a greater or lesser extent. In the Hymnbook you will find both approaches. The official texts of Sunday Evening Prayer and Night Prayer are given in full, but other material is included as well, and the order of Morning Prayer is less elaborate than the official one.

Why change the official rites? The answer is that they are rather complicated, and it seems preferable to celebrate a simpler version (which is faithful to the spirit of the original) rather than put people off altogether. There are good historical reasons for doing this. The liturgy in the present Divine Office books is of the Monastic type; and the monk's whole day is geared up to the celebration of the Office. But before monasteries even existed people were praying the Office, almost certainly using simpler forms which did not vary so much as the Monastic ones, and which could be memorised – the way we know most of the prayers of the Mass off by heart. In particular, the People's Office would have fewer psalms, whereas in some monasteries the whole psalter would be sung every week, or even every *day*.

The Celebration Hymnal offers a framework for Morning and Evening Prayer which can be varied as desired. As they differ slightly they will be dealt with separately.

Morning Prayer

To begin the first office of the day **Psalm 94(95)** is traditionally sung. As the first office provided in the book is Morning Prayer, it would be appropriate to start with this; either in a chant version (Gelineau or Murray, no 679) as a song with refrain (435, 783) or in the hymn version given on p.343. Before this 'invitatory psalm' the leader says or sings 'Lord, open our lips' and all respond as shown.

Other Invitatory Psalms are nos 23 (668) or 99 (no less than seven versions.)

Alternatively you may start Morning Prayer with the Introduction on p.344 (which also serves for Evening Prayer).

From then on the *basic* form of Morning Prayer is:

A hymn (1)

A psalm or psalms (and a canticle) (2)

A short reading and response (3)

A Gospel Canticle: The Benedictus (4)

Intercessions ending with Our Father

Blessing and conclusion

Notes:

(1) If Psalm 94 has already been sung a hymn may not be wanted as well. If a hymn *is* sung, it is useful in choosing it to take 'light' or the new day as the theme (e.g. Each morning with its new-born light, 446)(see Tunefinder).

(2) Morning Prayer used to have a 'praise' psalm (148, 149 or 150) every day. Psalm 148 is given here. You could sing it all together, in two groups, or have a cantor sing it with all with an antiphon after each verse. You could also sing a hymn. *Praise the Lord, ye heavens* (585) is based on Psalm 148; *O Praise ye the Lord* (244) is based on Psalm 150 with 'suggestions' from Ps 148; Ps 150 itself will be found at no. 692; and there is a metrical version of another praise psalm, Ps 116, at no. 53. *Surrexit Christus* (796) includes the words of the Canticle of the Three Children, which is in the Office for Morning Prayer of Sunday and would be an excellent choice.

If you want to have two psalms, the praise psalm could come second, preceded by one of the other traditional morning psalms found in the book: 62 (674, 778) or 42 (672). Psalm 50 (673) is always in the Office on Friday.

(3) Extensive Scripture reading is not a feature of most of the Hours. The readings given in the Office are never more than three or four verses. When choosing a reading, it would be a good idea to find one from that day's Office or Mass – i.e. related to the liturgy of the day. The **Response** could be replaced by a brief silence before the Benedictus.

(4) The Benedictus is no. 693. It could be sung with a response between verses.

Evening Prayer

Evening Prayer could begin in one of two ways:
- with the Introduction and hymn
- with the Light Service (lucernarium).

The second arrangement is not found in the Divine Office at present but it is something very ancient. As mentioned above in Morning Prayer, the symbolism of *light*, which marks the succession of day and night, is one of the most constant ideas in the Office. In the morning we welcome the sun, while in the evening we remind ourselves that although the sun is departing, we have a light which can never be extinguished, Christ.

This action originates from the custom of the lighting of lamps, an everyday occurrence in the households of ancient times, which was thus given an extra significance. In the modern liturgy it still occurs, and with great ceremony, at the Easter Vigil, but it is also found in old versions of the Office and in the second century Apostolic Tradition of Hippolytus (the source for our Eucharistic Prayer 2.) The text of the leader's Evening Thanksgiving (not found in the words edition of the hymnbook) is taken directly from Hippolytus. The hymn *O gracious light* is also very ancient – perhaps as early as the 2nd century AD.

After the candle or candles have been lit, some incense may be burnt while the psalm is sung with the response 'O Lord let my prayer rise before you...' This should be sung slowly and meditatively with the incense vividly symbolising the prayer which is the whole purpose of the Office.

Whether you have begun the Office this way, or more conventionally with the Introduction and Hymn, you should continue with a psalm or psalms, for from now on the structure of Evening Prayer resembles that of Morning Prayer.

The psalms for Sunday Evening Prayer from the Office are given on pp.347–349. The Revelation Canticle (hymn no 396) should follow them if you are following the book (a substitute in Lent is *Christ suffered for you*, no 418). But you may not want these psalms at all, in which case the table on p.116 should be consulted. Traditionally the Vespers psalms have been taken from those numbered from 109 on, and suitable ones would be 120, 121, 125, 135, 138. If you have two, it would be a good idea to have a meditative one (e.g. 120, 138) followed by a joyful one (121, 125, 135). Note: you need not limit your choice to these – look through the whole table before choosing. Note also that some of the Taizé chants are actually settings of the psalms, the verses of which are sung by a cantor while everyone else is singing a refrain.

The Gospel Canticle at Evening Prayer is the Magnificat, and there are five settings to choose from: the one given in the full music and melody editions at this point, plus nos 414, 479, 694, 749.

Night Prayer

Night Prayer is more straightforward than the other hours and the texts given in the book are more or less straight from the Divine Office, for Sunday. Ps 90(91) is the most familiar Night Prayer psalm. Note that there is another setting of the Night Prayer hymn at no. 564.

4. MUSIC FOR THE SACRAMENTS
and Other Rites

The Sacraments are moments of special meeting between God and his people. They may be repeated frequently, like the Eucharist, or they may take place only at important or solemn moments of life: birth, marriage, old age and sickness.

It is Christ who is acting in the sacraments and in each of them there is some 'outward sign' by which we recognise his presence: the bread and wine of the eucharist, the water of baptism, the oil of the sick, the couple themselves in marriage.

The sacraments are celebrations of the *whole* Church, and (though they are often family occasions as well) not private affairs.

Nowadays more and more parishes have preparation programmes for the candidates, but so far this is limited mainly to the sacraments of initiation, with which this brief survey will start.

Christian Initiation

Although it is not the most frequent occurrence in parish life, the baptism of an unbaptized adult and the whole process leading up to it are taken as the norm of Christian Initiation, on which all other forms are based. It is known from its initials as RCIA.

The last command of the Lord was to go and make disciples of all nations. The Church and every individual Christian must always keep this command in mind, and a parish must make it a duty to bring more of God's children to his banquet, by calling them to conversion.

The great difference between the RCIA, which became the official rite in 1988, and what preceded it, is in the length of time which it sets aside for preparation. This is divided into several stages, as follows:

Period of Evangelisation and pre-Catechumenate – when people, feeling the first stirrings of faith, are making their first enquiries about the Church. This period is of indeterminate length. It ends with a definite commitment marked by the *Rite of Acceptance into the Order of Catechumens* which takes place at a time to be decided by each community.

Period of Catechumenate when the faith of the candidates is nurtured and grows. Its length is determined by the progress of each individual. It comes to an end in its turn with the *Rite of Election*, which usually takes place in the Cathedral on the 1st Sunday of Lent. The catechumens become 'the elect' and prepare for the sacraments at Easter.

Period of Purification and Enlightenment. This is the time leading up to baptism, usually the season of Lent. It is a time of reflection and deepening of faith, and is punctuated by the Scrutinies and other rites (see Sundays of Lent 3–5). It leads up to the climax of the whole process, the *Celebration of the Sacraments of Initiation*, for which the proper time is the Easter Vigil.

Period of Postbaptismal Catechesis (Mystagogia). This is the time following the celebration of the sacraments when the new Christians experience full membership of the community, by means of catechesis and sharing in the Eucharist.

Infant Baptism
Although RCIA is the norm, infant baptism is the more common event. But the way that adults become christian – by hearing the word, experiencing conversion, deepening their faith

and making a commitment – is a process which everyone has to undergo, although events may not happen in this order. Those baptized as children have some catching up to do later, and the whole community can share in the progress of the catechumens and renew their own commitment with them each Lent and Easter.

Confirmation

This is the second stage of initiation in the 'ideal' pattern of the RCIA, and received at the same time as baptism. Children are usually confirmed in their early teens and the occasion is seen as a renewal of commitment and a way of conferring strength for the journey to full maturity.

Reception of a baptized person into full communion with the Catholic Church

This event ('reception of a convert') may be more common in most British parishes than adult baptism. It may be prepared for by a process akin to the catechumenate although the two should not be confused. Often the prospective Catholic is a person of deep faith and Christian formation and does not need a long preparation; each person has their individual requirements.

First Communion

Reception of the Eucharist is the highest stage of initiation and the newly-baptized and confirmed adults receive the Eucharist at the Mass when they are initiated. Children have to be prepared, and this process and the final celebration are usually watched with interest by the parish.

All the stages of initiation involve liturgical celebrations, and the parish musicians should be involved in them. It often gets left to catechists and schoolteachers to arrange everything, even though music may not be their particular expertise; but it is the place of the musicians to look after the music, and so they should be familiar with the rites, ready with suggestions for music and able to animate the celebrations.

Penance and Reconciliation

The public celebration of this sacrament takes place in many parishes in Lent and Advent, usually consisting of a liturgy of the word or something similar, followed by individual confessions. The parish choir or singing group can add considerably to the success of such celebrations.

Worship of the Eucharist outside Mass

This is not so frequent as before 1970, and it has gone largely unnoticed that the rites of 'benediction' were revised in the mid-70s. Benediction is in fact only one part of the pattern of liturgical celebration found in the new liturgical books, which envisage an act of worship with the following elements:
– Exposition
– Period of adoration (extended as long as required, with readings, prayers and songs)
– Benediction
– Reposition of the Blessed Sacrament and conclusion.
  The modern emphasis on the Mass has coloured our view of the Eucharist and we can understand the insistence of the Vatican Council that devotion to the Blessed Sacrament should be seen in relation to the Mass. The original and still the first purpose of Reservation of the Blessed Sacrament is to distribute to the sick and as viaticum. In contemplating Christ in the Eucharist, therefore, it is not simply his presence which should occupy our mind but the memory of all the great works of redemption accomplished by our Saviour, and the great promises he has made to us of which the Eucharist is a pledge.

Marriage

Choosing music for weddings is something very personal, although it should be kept in mind (as said above) that a wedding is a celebration of the whole church and not just of the couple. The wedding is a public sign of a Marriage, a relationship which does not start or finish with the celebration but enters a new stage with it.

The couple (and families) may have a clear idea of what music they want, or they may appreciate a list of suggestions. Each couple is different and the list on page 106 cannot hope to include everybody's favourite hymn. Rather, it aims to present a wide selection of hymns and songs which have a particular reference to the texts of the Rite or the Christian view of marriage.

As a long-term consideration, it would be a good idea for the parish musicians (especially choir and cantors) to assemble a repertoire of liturgically-based music (such as Responsorial Psalms, Gospel Acclamations and Mass chants) which can be offered as suggestions to couples, together with the promise of leadership and support in the celebration itself. Weddings, especially at Mass, are in danger of becoming 'hymn-sandwiches' to the detriment of the liturgy.

However, such advice should not be heavy-handed. A wedding is one of the few occasions when ordinary people are privileged to help plan, and take a leading part in, a liturgy and it may not be the moment to embark on an extensive course in liturgical education. The ground-work should have been done already.

Anointing the Sick

The sacrament of the sick was until quite recently given only to those near death. The Vatican Council however asked that it be revised to show that it is 'not a sacrament for those only who are at the point of death... as soon as any one of the faithful begins to be in danger of death from sickness or old age, the fitting time for that person to receive this sacrament has arrived' (Liturgy Constitution, 73). Viaticum and the 'last rites' are given where appropriate, but in general Anointing is thus now a sacrament 'for the seriously ill', and may be received more than once; the prayers ask for healing in mind, body and spirit.

Like the other sacraments it may be celebrated during Mass, and the parish can be made aware of the presence of sick people and the duty to care for them by an occasional Anointing Mass. Such celebrations are invariably a source of spiritual riches and healing for all present.

The parish can be regularly reminded of its sick members by seeing the sending out of the Eucharistic Ministers each Sunday bearing the Eucharist for the sick.

The Rite of Funerals

Choosing music for funerals faces some of the same problems as for weddings, since this is another occasion when ordinary people are asked to help in the planning of a liturgy. The parallel goes further, in that these are people who are under the stress of strong emotion. They may not be able to give their undivided attention to the task of choosing music. At the same time they will want to be faithful to the dead person's memory, and so will probably expect both the freedom to choose hymns, and a range of suggestions.

The list on p.108 does not claim to anticipate everyone's needs but aims to include a wide selection of hymns and songs which have a particular reference to the texts of the Rite and the Christian view of death.

As at Weddings, but probably more acutely, the choice of music will be limited by what the participants will know and what musical resources are available. See the suggestion in the Marriage Rite section that the parish musicians take a hand in assembling a repertoire of music for sacramental occasions, and even offering practical help.

This could be a task for retired people who are also musicians and who are able to attend funerals during the week. The presence of a 'funeral choir' of even two or three people who can start and support the singing would be a great service to the people present.

The best time for learning funeral music, as for any other special category of music, is during the year in the general course of celebration. If the parish repertoire is rich enough it should contain music which will be of use at funerals. Those in charge of choosing the music should look through the suggestions on p.108 and see when they can be incorporated into general use and so become familiar.

The new Order of Christian Funerals contains rites in several stages.

Prayer after death: which could be led by the priest on his first visit to the bereaved family, in home or at the hospital. There are other forms of prayer as well, and any of them could be led by family members.

Vigil for the deceased: this will bring thoughts of a 'wake', but it could take place in a church, either in the presence of the body or not. It contains a Liturgy of the Word and several opportunities for singing.

Reception of the Body: a rite is provided for the arrival of the body at the Church, which may take place separately from the Funeral Mass. Singing is a feature of this rite as well.

Mass: The usual principles apply to singing at a funeral mass, namely the avoidance of the hymn-sandwich. If this is to be done, however, singers are needed (see above). A simple psalm response, alleluia and set of Eucharistic acclamations are desirable. The Song of Farewell at the end of the Rite is an important musical item.

The liturgy ends with the **Commital and burial** which presents practical problems for music. However, if the whole Funeral Rite takes place in a crematorium or cemetry chapel, it is important to provide music, particularly for the Liturgy of the Word and the Song of Farewell.

5. MUSIC IN PRACTICE: A CHAPTER FOR LEADERS

The aim of this brief guide to the Mass, the Office, the Sacraments and the Liturgical Year has been to emphasise the need to plan the liturgy with understanding, so that appropriate words of praise and proclamation are put on people's lips.

Everything stands or falls, though, by how it works in practice. Most people *will* sing, if only they are given leadership. Just as when you plan the music you need constantly to remind yourself that *the needs of the whole assembly come first,* so when leading worship you have to aim to help people to sing and not – as sometimes happens – hinder them.

For God to praised worthily, people need not only the right words and the right music but the right 'invitation' to sing and the right support while they are doing it. No matter how well-chosen and well-performed (from your point of view) the music may be, if people can't join in it doesn't work. If people don't sing for us, we may put it down to the perverseness of the average congregation. Nine times out of ten it is because the leader (who may be an organist, a cantor, a guitarist, or a whole group of people) is doing something wrong.

But when it all goes right, the liturgy will really *belong* to everybody, they will be interested in ever greater participation, and will probably start coming to Mass on time. To make all this happen is the minstry of musicians.

Knowledge – experience

You need two things to help you develop the skills of a music minister – knowledge and experience. This Introduction, and your own further reading, will impart a little knowledge. Some things, though, only come with experience, for example:

* knowing what makes people sing
* knowing how people learn new music
* knowing how much new music people can take at one time, and thus
* knowing how to plan to introduce new music at people's pace, not yours
* knowing how to blend the old and the new, the familiar and the unfamiliar (about 95% to 5%)
* knowing how to choose songs of the right length
* knowing how to choose songs of the right mood (so that people can *praise* at the appropriate moment, *reflect* at another and so on)
* knowing the value and place of *silence*

- and two more which are less easy to describe:
* knowing how and whether to persevere with something which you believe in but which didn't work first time
* knowing how and when to *challenge* people with something out of the ordinary, either in words or music

Do you like your congregation?

It helps if the music-leader *likes* people, rather than looking on them as an awkward and intractable lot. After all, they may think the same about you. You are doing something at *their* mass and you have to justify your existence. Even more galling, they may not even notice you!

Never forget that it is the *assembly as a whole* which is the 'singer' of the Mass – not the cantor, or the choir, but everybody.

Helping people to sing

People need to be helped to overcome their reticence about singing in public. The highest motivations for singing are faith and the love of God, and it will help you to keep these spiritual motives in mind, to give a sense of purpose to what you do which may communicate itself to other people.

Having said that, your main way of helping people to sing will be simply to treat them with respect, even to *love* them. There are ways of asking people to do things. Although you may have only what you consider an average success rate to start with, people will sing if you get the conditions right.

Here are some of the conditions.

Music that sounds right.
By this is meant music that people like, or will like on acquaintance. Most people, and so most Catholics, have a 'middle-of-the-road' taste in music which as far as what they hear in Church is concerned, would embrace hymns and Christmas carols and modern songs that are not too 'way out', such as *Follow me* or *Sing of the Lord's goodness*. People should have little difficult in responding to these songs.

But you should aim to extend people's experience as well. A more exotic sound, either ancient (e.g. nos 732 or 750); modern and rhythmic (e.g. 821 or 827); or modern 'art' music (748 or 756) might not be be absorbed or welcomed at once, but if you believe in them you can find ways of using any of these songs.

Here is a further selection of more 'difficult' songs you may have overlooked:
402 As long as men on earth

25

406 Bartimaeus
419 By the cross
423 Christ has arisen, alleluia
431 Christ our pasch
443 Divided our pathways
470 Give praise to the Lord
482 God most high of all creation
496 He's a most unusual man
499 His light now shines
505 I lift up my eyes
545 Lord, in everything I do
571 O what a gift
576 One day will come
578 Our help is the name of the Lord
586 Praise to the Lord
660 You, Israel, return now
739 Father, we come to you
806 Wake your power

Actually, for some congregations almost anything sounds strange or exotic if there is a history of non-singing. But you may be surprised at what people like and dislike, which doesn't always correspond to what you think will happen.

Music that sounds singable
This often amounts to the same point as the previous one, though seen from another angle. Music can be made to sound *too difficult* when in fact it is nothing of the kind. This can happen if a tune is played or sung with elaborate accompaniment.

If you want people to absorb music unconsciously, by hearing it sung or played during Mass before you are going to ask them to join in, a convincing performance by the choir or whoever is essential. But if you are teaching directly, use only your voice and gestures.

So music you want to teach should be:

Music that you can teach
You should be able to sing it yourself, in front of other people, with confidence. You should be enthusiastic and not apologetic about it. Teach a tune in sections, maybe a line at a time. If a tune has two or more lines the same,

you can point this out, but don't use musical jargon. Sing in a clear voice which doesn't sound intimidating but invites people to repeat it and gives them the confidence that they can do as well as you.

Don't tell people off. If they don't get it right first time, ask them to listen again and repeat – don't zero in on the mistake.

Get to learn how much new music people can absorb.

Get to learn how long people take to retain a new tune. You may teach a Holy, holy and find people have forgotten it by the time they have to sing it. Next time, give them a little more help.

Music that carries a meaning
You have to make people see the liturgical and spiritual purpose in learning it. For a 'hymn-sandwich' congregation, as has been said, anything other than a hymn (e.g. a Psalm, Gospel Acclamation or Holy Holy) may seem foreign at first.

Show, therefore, that singing a 'Holy, holy' is going to enhance the Mass (the clergy have to believe this as well!)

Music at the right time
Don't ask people to sing something at variance with their mood at the time. The time of day has an influence – 9 am as opposed to 11 (people can't sing so high earlier in the day). On the other hand, don't dampen people's enthusiasm by a quiet song when an extrovert one is needed.

You can't always gauge exactly what people are going to want, but you can acquire experience; this can be helped by keeping notes of what worked, what didn't, and why.

Too long – too short; too loud – too soft; familiar – unfamiliar; song – silence: these are some of the oppositions which have to be balanced up. But don't let them become an obsession. In the end, God will speak through the music, not you; and sometimes He speaks in totally surprising ways, which you did not plan.

Part Two: The Hymn Planner

There is more than one reason for choosing a hymn to sing at Mass, but in the case of the lists which form the bulk of this book the first consideration has been THE SUITABILITY OF THEIR TEXTS, i.e. not just because of their nice tunes.

Have a good look at the hymns suggested; don't dismiss a song because you don't know or don't like the tune. There are some very good hymn texts which get regularly overlooked for this reason, but you can often find a substitute tune by using the Metrical Index or the Tunefinder (pp.113,109).

Only suggestions

Sometimes a suggestion is made (such as Entrance/Gathering, E/G) as to how a particular hymn might be used. The suggestions are not meant to be taken as rigid rules and you should exercise your own judgment.

As a further way of involving yourself personally in the planning of the liturgy, you should see if you can improve on the selections given. Undoubtedly you will find some better ones from time to time. Space is given after each Sunday for you to record your own choice, including any new ideas.

Extra hymns

What happens if you need three hymns and there are only two well-known ones on the list?

First of all, look at the General Eucharistic Songs section (p.28). Not every hymn has to have an explicit reference to the Sunday's Gospel and you can, for example, sing an entrance hymn which expresses
- **gathering** *We gather together* (345 or 644);

What is this place (818); *Gather us in* (752), or
- **Sunday** *Again the Lord's own day is here*, (386), or
- **people of God** *All people that on earth do dwell* (11).

A hymn for the Preparation of the Gifts could be one of personal dedication (*My God accept my heart this day*) as the old 'Offertory' hymns are not so appropriate today, when the Eucharistic prayer is proclaimed aloud. It may be decided that no singing is needed here at all.

A communion thanksgiving or final hymn should be one of optimism and hope: (*Sing to the world of Christ*, (605) or Mission (*Forth in the peace of Christ*, (78 or 744)).

You must, of course, guard against choosing wildly inappropriate words; it is advisable to read through a hymn you choose if it has been some time since you sang it.

You will also find in the Index categories such as 'Discipleship' or 'Love of others' which you can relate to the readings of the day. Always make a note of your choices; you will find this invaluable the next time the Sunday comes round.

Spreading out your learning

Be adventurous in your choice, and extend the repertoire of your congregation. With this book in front of you, you have the chance of planning a long time ahead. You can plan to introduce, say, five new hymns in the course of a year. See where your choice occurs in the lists – sometimes hymns are suggested two or more weeks running. Having introduced a new hymn, repeat it quite soon and then after a slightly longer interval.

GENERAL EUCHARIST SONGS

ENTRANCE/GATHERING

Extended gathering songs:
Veni sancte Spiritus (esp. Pentecost) 638
Adoramus te, Domine 696
Jubilate Deo 707
Ostende nobis Domine (esp. Advent) 711
Bless the Lord, my soul 728
Confitemini Domino 735
In the Lord 759
Psallite Domino 790

Psalms and songs with chorus
Open your ears 242
We celebrate this festive day 344
We gather together 345
All the earth, proclaim 390
All you nations 391
Come, let us sing out our joy 435
Gather, Christians 467
He is risen, Alleluia 494
O be joyful in the Lord 565
Our help is the name of the Lord 578
Praise to the Lord, praise him 586
Sing to the Lord a song 602
Sing to the Lord 604
The light of Christ 614
This is the day 625
Arise, come to your God (Ps 99 (100)) 680
Gather us in 752
Sing of the Lord's goodness 794
You are the Lord 822

Other songs
All people that on earth do dwell 10
At the name of Jesus 28
Holy God, we praise thy name 121
Holy, holy, holy 122/3
Immortal, invisible 134
O worship the King 253
Again the Lord's own day 386
Awake, awake! 405
Father, we praise you 455
We gather together to ask 644
Come, rejoice 731
Jubilate everybody 766
Sing all creation 793
What is this place? 818

BLESSING OF WATER
Water of Life
Christ the Lord has come 430
There is one Lord 621
A pure heart (Ps 50(51)) 673
In the abundance 757

PREPARATION OF THE GIFTS
All that I am 11
Almighty Father, Lord most high 17
Almighty Father, take this bread 18
Come, Lord Jesus 51
Fill my house 74
In bread we bring you, Lord 135
Let all mortal flesh 166
O God, we give ourselves today 224
O holy Lord, by all adored 228
O King of might and splendour 234
Praise to the Lord 264
Reap me the earth 268
Take my hands 296
Take our bread 297
We are gathering together 341
We bring our gifts 343
What can we offer you? 351
Blest are you 410
Father, I place into your hands 450
Gifts of bread and wine 469
God gives us harvest 478
Lord of creation 547
Sing everyone a song 600
Son of the Father 607
Take my life 608
Upon this table, Lord 637
Welcome, all ye noble saints 638
Ps 42(43): I will go to the altar 672
Ps 83(84) My soul is longing 675
Ps 121(122) I rejoiced 687
I rejoiced 755
With open hands 821

COMMUNION
Pre-Communion/ Processional
Lamb of God, settings 2–4

Communion Procession
As one body 403
Ps 22(23): My shepherd is the Lord 667
Ps 41(42): My soul is thirsting 671
Adoramus te, Domine 696
Now in this banquet 774
O Christe Domine Jesu 777
Unless a grain 812

Communion Thanksgiving
Alleluia! sing to Jesus 7
Draw nigh and take 65
In Christ there is no east or west 128
Into one we all are gathered 139
Lord Jesus Christ 179
Now thank we all our God 211
O thou who at thy Eucharist 249
Praise we our God with joy 266
This is my will 327
Where is love 358
An upper room 399
Before Christ died 408
I am the bread of life 501
Jesus the Lord said 523
Let us talents and tongues 535
Lord, enthroned in heavenly 543
O food of travellers 567
Shepherd of souls 597
Sing to the world of Christ 605
Tell out, my soul 609
Thine be the glory (Easter) 622
This is my body 623
When the time came 653
Ps 26(27): One thing I ask 670
Ps 114(115): How can I repay 686
Ps 135(136): O give thanks 690
I received the living God 754
Jesus, Lord of life and love 764
Praise now your God 787
Those who were in the dark 802
You are the Lord 822

RECESSIONAL
Forth in the peace of Christ 78/744
Forth in the name 79
Go tell everyone 99
I will be with you 510
The Spirit lives to set us free 618

EXIT PROCESSIONAL
With a song in our heart 361
Go out to the whole world 703
Jubilate Deo 706/7
Surrexit Christus 796
You shall go out with joy 823

YEAR A: ADVENT TO PENTECOST

Advent-Christmastide, Year A

There are two aspects to Advent. In the early part of the season, in all three cycles, the prayers and readings are concerned with the second coming of Christ. As Christmas approaches, however, we naturally think more about commemorating the first coming. But even on Christmas night we sing 'Christ has died, Christ is risen, Christ will come again', because for Christians the past, the present and the future are inseparable. We cannot look at the baby without thinking of Jesus the man. And we cannot think of Jesus the man without thinking of Jesus in glory at the Father's right hand.

So in the first Gospel of Advent (1st Sunday) we hear 'stand ready, because the Son of Man is coming at an hour you do not expect,' and the psalm says 'I rejoiced when I heard them say, Let us go to God's house'. Everything that has happened so far in history is a preparation, leading up to the time when we all hope to be living with God.

The First Readings in Advent Year A are all taken from Isaiah, the 'Advent prophet'. They are full of joy. Advent is called a penitential season, but this is because we are waiting for something wonderful to happen and want to have a clear mind, not because we want to spend time bewailing our faults.

The Second Readings are taken from Romans, except on the 3rd Sunday which is from St James.

The Gospels give the four Sundays of Advent their traditional character. (As this is Year A they are all taken from Matthew). Here is the scheme of Gospels for the whole season, to give a comprehensive view:

Sunday 1: The judgement and the end of time (Mt 24:37–49)
      2: John the Baptist calls us to repent (Mt 3:1–2)
      3: John as the fore-runner of Christ (Mt 11:2–11)
      4: The coming birth of Jesus (Mt 1:18–24)
Christmas Midnight: the birth of Jesus (Luke 2:1–14)
Christmas Day: John's prologue, 'In the beginning was the word' (Jn 1:1–18)
Holy Family: The flight into Egypt (Mt 2:13–15, 19–23)
January 1st (Solemnity of Mary, Mother of God):
      The naming of Jesus (Luke 2:16–21)
2nd Sunday of Christmas: as Christmas Day
Epiphany: The wise men come from the East (Mt 2:1–12)
Baptism of the Lord: Jesus is baptised in the Jordan by John (Mt 3:13–17)

NOTES

1. Asterisked hymns may be used on more than one Sunday in a particular season.
2. Some hymns are based on one or other of the Readings of the day and these are noted as follows: 1R = First Reading; 2R = Second Reading; Gosp = Gospel;
3. Suggestions for the use of the hymns at Mass are noted thus (note that these are *suggestions* only): E/G = Entrance/Gathering; PG = Preparation of Gifts; Comm = Communion; R = Recessional, CT/R = Communion Thanksgiving or Recessional.
4. If you need EXTRA HYMNS: see p.27
5. Learning NEW HYMNS: see p.24
6. Space is provided after each Sunday for your own choice of hymns. Good ideas should be written down straight away so they are not forgotten.

Advent-Christmastide Hymns, Year A

Advent 1 *Stand ready because the Son of Man is coming*
Isaiah 2:1–5; Ps 121(122); Rom 13:11–14; MATTHEW 24:37–44

- 45 Colours of day (R)
- 61 Dear maker of the starry skies (v5 cf Gosp) (E/G)
- 112 Hark! a herald voice (vv1,2: 2R) (E/G)
- 166 Let all mortal flesh (v3: 2R) PG
- 233 O Jesus Christ, remember (Gosp)
- 242 Open your ears (E/G)
- 342 We are gathering together (PG)
- ★384 Abba Father send your Spirit (+ optional Advent verses)
- 480 God is working his purpose out (Gosp)
- 613 The king shall come (E/G)

- 639 Wake! awake! (Gosp)
- 640 Wake up! The dawn is near
- 687 Cf Responsorial Psalm
- 704 (round) I rejoiced
- 711 Ostende nobis (cf Gosp Acc) (E/G)
- ★733 Come to set us free (E/G)
- ★742 My soul in stillness
- 755 I rejoiced
- ★777 O Christe Domine Jesu (+ Ps 84)
- ★805 Wait for the Lord
- ★810 We have a King who comes in glory
- AK 35 (Resp Ps), ★45 (Gosp Acc)

Your choice....

Advent 2 *Prepare a way for the Lord, make his paths straight and all mankind shall see the salvation of God*
Isaiah 11:1–10; Ps 71(72); Romans 15:4–9; MATTHEW 3:1–12

- 16 A voice cries = AK71
- 110 Hail to the Lord's anointed (CT/R)
- 182 Lord, we pray for golden peace
- 239 On Jordan's bank (E/G)
- 385 Across the years (E/G)
- 498 Hills of the north (CT/R)
- 500 Our God reigns (CT/R)
- 531 Lest he be too far

- 540 Look around you (Pen. rite)
- 560 O comfort my people (E/G)
- ★739 Father, we come to you (E/G)
- 770 My people, I hear you calling
- 789 Prepare ye the way
- 806 Wake your power (CT/R)
- Ak24 (Resp Ps), ★45, 71

Your choice....

Advent 3 *The eyes of the blind shall be opened*
Isaiah 35:1–6,10; Ps 145; James 5:7–10; MATTHEW 11:2–112

- 43 Christ is our king
- 110 Hail to the Lord's anointed
- 239 On Jordan's bank (E/G)
- 267 Promised Lord and Christ is he (CT/R)
- 310 The King of glory comes
- 319 The Spirit of the Lord (cf Gosp Acc)
- 345 We gather together (E/G)
- 405 Awake, awake! fling off the night
- 436 Come, Lord Jesus
- 439 Come, thou long-expected Jesus

- 537 Like a sea without a shore
- 563 Now watch for God's coming (2R)
- 664 The eyes of the blind (1R)
- 676 Psalm 84 (Resp.Ps) Resp.2 is today's Response. The verses can be adapted.
- 749 Great is the Lord
- 800 The voice of God goes out
- 820 When the King shall come
- 823 You shall go out with joy
- AK 39 (cf Resp Ps), ★45

Your choice....

Advent 4 *The virgin will conceive and give birth to a son'*
Isaiah 7:10–14; Ps 23:1–6; Romans 1:1–7; MATTHEW 1:18–24

110 Hail to the Lord's anointed	611 The Angel Gabriel
216 O come, O come, Emmanuel (E/G)	613 The King shall come
301 The coming of our God	686 Psalm 23 (24) (cf Resp Psalm)
381 A noble flower of Judah	732 Come, Saviour, come (E/G; also Pen.Rite)
382 A sign is seen in heaven	742 For you, O Lord
437 Come, O divine Messiah	*759 In the Lord (E/G; Comm)
465 Freely I give to you	AK14 (cf Resp Ps), *45, 74
587 Rain down justice	

Your choice....

Christmas

Christmas hymns are listed in the Words edition (p.365) and in any case people will have plenty of ideas about what they want to sing today. But it is worth spending a moment to take a closer look at what the hymns and carols actually say, because even at Christmas what you sing at Mass has to *mean* something.

What to look for is the *category* of each carol. It may be:

1. Narrative:

The angel Gabriel (cf. Luke 1:26 ff).　　The first Nowell (cf. Luke 2:8ff; Matt 2:1, 9ff)

While shepherds watched (cf. Luke 2:8 ff)　　God rest ye merry, gentlemen (cf. Luke 1:4 ff)

2. Theological and Reflective

Once in royal David's city　　　　　Of the Father's love begotten

See amid the winter's snow　　　　I wonder as I wander

Hark, the herald angels sing　　　　It came upon the midnight clear

O come, all ye faithful　　　　　　A noble flower of Juda

O little town of Bethlehem

3. Picturesque

Silent night　　　　　　　　　　Ding dong! merrily on high

Come to the manger　　　　　　　Away in a manger

(4. Legendary: such as *I saw three ships*, or *Good King Wenceslas*, neither of which are in the book. We three kings is mainly legendary.)

You should be able to work out others for yourself (although some carols, including some of those above, could come in more than one category). And having done so, make a good balance between the picturesque, even though this category contains most of the favourite carols, and those with a more solid content.

Note the differences between Midnight Mass and the Day Mass. On Christmas Day the Gospel (John 1:1–18) is more 'theological' than at Midnight, and you could keep *O come all ye faithful* for the morning; *Hark the herald angels* sing would be a suitably joyful finale for Midnight Mass.

The **Gloria** is closely connected with Christmas, as the first two lines are actually from the Christmas gospel. The Taizé Gloria (Eucharist section) has special Christmas words. You might consider singing 21 *Angels we have heard in heaven* as a Gloria.

Another Christmas text is Psalm 97 (98), and there are three settings to choose from, nos 724, 772 and 792.

Finally, you might look at some lesser known or new pieces which you may not have noticed:

147	I wonder as I wander	524	Jesus the Word has lived among us
378	A child is born in Bethlehem	705	Jesus Christ, little lord (round)
381	A noble flower of Juda	725	Awake, awake
465	Freely I give to you	790	Psallite Domino
507	I saw a star		AK29, 72, 75

CHRISTMAS READINGS

Midnight Mass: Isaiah 9:1–7; Ps 95(96); Titus 2:11–14; LUKE 2:1–14
Dawn Mass: Isaiah 62:11–12; Ps 96(97); Titus 3:4–7; LUKE 2:15–20
Day Mass: Isaiah 52:7–10; Ps 97(98) (several settings to choose from); Hebrews 1:1–6; JOHN 1:1–18 (or 1–5,9–14)

Your Christmas Choice:

Holy Family
Help us to live as the Holy Family,
united in respect and love (Opening Prayer)
Ecclus 3:2–6,12–14; Ps 127(128); Col 3:12–21; MATTHEW 2:13–15,19–23

18	Almighty Father, take this bread (PG)	238	Once in royal David's city
21	Angels we have heard (Gloria)	240	On this house your blessing
127	How dark was the stable	281	Sing of Mary, pure and lowly
137	In the bleak midwinter	507	I saw a star
139	Into one we all are gathered (PG)	568	O Lady, full of God's own grace
157	Jesus my Lord, my God (see v.3)	649	What child is this
179	Lord Jesus Christ	785	One shall tell another
181	Lord of all hopefulness	786	Peace I give

Your choice....

The Mother of God
When the appointed time came, God sent his Son, born of a woman
Numbers 6:22–27; Ps 66(67); Gal 4:4–7; LUKE 2:16–21

126	Holy Virgin, by God's decree	382	A sign is seen in heaven
192	Mary Immaculate	492	Hail Mary, Mother of our God
281	Sing of Mary (E/G)	555	Mother of Jesus
315	The race that long in darkness pined	568	O Lady, full of God's own grace
339	Virgin wholly marvellous	572	Of one that is so fair and bright
356	Where are you bound	611	The angel Gabriel (E/G)
365	Ye who own the faith of Jesus	749	Great is the Lord (CT/R)
381	A noble flow'r of Juda		AK74

Your choice....

2nd Sunday after Christmas *The word was made flesh, and dwelt among us.*

Ecclus 24:1–2,8–12; Ps 147; Eph 1:3–6,15–18; JOHN 1:1–18 (or 1–5.9–14)

General Christmastide, also:

92	Go, tell it on the mountain	571	(v 1–3) Oh what a gift
97	God is love, his the care	573	Of the Father's love begotten (E/G)
175	Long ago in Bethlehem	605	Sing to the world (CT/R)
306	The God whom earth and sea and sky	610	That which we have heard
315	The race that long in darkness	614	The light of Christ (Gosp.)
483	God our maker, mighty Father (see Tunefinder)	629	Thou whose almighty Word (Gosp.)
509	I was born before creation (1R)	633	To God our Father be the praise
518	In the beginning all was empty	724	All the ends of the earth
524	Jesus the Word has lived among us	747	God who spoke in the beginning (see Tunefinder)
551	Love came down at Christmas	802	Those who were in the dark (CT/R)

Your choice....

The Epiphany *The nations come to your light and kings to your dawning brightness.*

Isaiah 60:1–6; Ps 71(72); Eph 3:2–3,5–6; MATTHEW 2:1–12

24	As with gladness men of old	507	I saw a star
34	Bethlehem, of noblest cities	605	Sing to the world of Christ
286	Songs of thankfulness and praise	648	Welcome all ye noble saints (Comm)
305	The first Nowell	649	What child is this
315	The race that long in darkness pined (E/G)	724	All the ends of the earth (E/G)
349	We three kings	772	New songs of celebration (E/G)
377	A child is born for us today	792	Sing a new song (E/G)
378	A child is born in Bethlehem	AK29	

Your choice....

The Baptism of the Lord *This is my beloved Son; my favour rests on him.*

Isaiah 42:1–4,6–7; Ps 28(29); Acts 10:34–38; MATTHEW 3:13–17

The Rite of Blessing of Water is suitable today, using:

Water of Life (Eucharist section)

430 Christ the Lord has come to save his people

also

110	Hail to the Lord's anointed	619	The Spirit of God rests upon me
242	Open your ears	651	When Jesus comes to be baptized (See Tunefinder)
286	Songs of thankfulness	772	New songs of celebration
315	The race that long in darkness pined (E/G)	792	Sing a new song
319	The Spirit of the Lord	800	The voice of God
518	In the beginning	819	When John baptized
524	Jesus the Lord has lived among us	820	When the King shall come again
594	(1–4) Send forth your spirit	AK24	

Your choice....

Lent and Eastertide, Year A

This season has been called 'the season of John'. This explains why, though there are four Gospels, there is only a three-year cycle. Out of eighteen Sundays and feasts from Lent 1 to Pentecost, twelve Gospels are from John. In particular there are the Passion on Good Friday and the three last Sundays of Lent, about which the Introduction to the Lectionary says: *the tradition of both East and West has been preserved by which the Gospel of John is read in the final weeks of Lent and throughout Easter time, because it is the 'spiritual' Gospel in which the mystery of Christ is sounded out to greater deapths (74).*

On the three Lent Sundays mentioned the Gospels are:

3: John 4:5–42 The Samaritan woman
4. John 9:1–41 The man born blind
5. John 11:1–45 The raising of Lazarus.

They can only be fully understood when it is realised they are connected with the RCIA (Rite of Christian Initiation of Adults), and any candidates in the parish will be making their final preparation for baptism. On the 1st Sunday of Lent, at the Cathedral, there is the Rite of Election, when the Bishop, as pastor of the local church, welcomes the candidates and they change from being 'catechumens' to 'elect'. On Sundays 3, 4, and 5, at the principal Sunday Mass in the parish, there are the three **Scrutinies,** which are 'rites for self-searching', when 'all that is weak, defective or sinful' is healed and all that is upright and good is strengthened. These rites take place after the Gospel and consist of prayers and intercessions, and a suitable song should be found to go with them. The texts may be found in the current editions of the **Parish Mass Book,** Year A, B or C part 1. The three Gospels mentioned above give great examples of conversion or healing and they are used as the basis of the special Prayers.

Even if there are no candidates for Baptism in the community, every Christian and so each parish should reflect on the meaning of 'dying and rising with Christ', and how Jesus by his passion, death and resurrection conquered sin, opened for us the gate of heaven and brought us together into the Church.

The first two Sundays of Lent are always concerned with Jesus' temptation in the desert (1) and his Transfiguration (2). Other Gospels in this season which are invariable are those of the Sunday after Easter ('doubting Thomas', Jn 20:19–31), and Pentecost (the gift of the Holy Spirit), which is actually a shorter version of the same passage (Jn 20:19–23).

In Eastertide the First Readings are always from the Acts of the Apostles and tell of the new-born Church preaching its risen Lord. In Year A the second readings are mostly from the 1st Letter of Peter, supposedly written as an instruction for the newly-baptised.

Ash Wednesday *Have mercy on us, Lord, for we have sinned*

Joel 2:12–18; Ps 50(51); 2 Cor 5:20–6:2; MATTHEW 6:1–6,16–18

25 Attend and keep this happy fast (see Tunefinder)	577 Our Father, we have wandered
81 From the deep I lift my voice	590 Remember, man, that you are dust (Ashes)
82 From the depths	660 You, Israel, return now
160 Keep we the fast	673 Psalm 50 (51) (Resp. Ps)
183 Lord, who throughout these forty days	★757 In the abundance
443 Divided our pathways	★780 O Lord, be not mindful (Pen Rite/Ashes)
454 Father of heaven	AK20 (Resp Ps)

Your choice....

Lent 1 *We do not live on bread alone.*
Genesis 2:7–9; 3:1–7; Ps 50(51); Rom 5:12–9 (or 12.17–9); MATTHEW 4:1–11

See Ash Wednesday; also
- 80 Forty days and forty nights
- 128 I am the bread of life (Comm)
- 165 Lead us, heavenly Father, lead us
- 180 Lord Jesus, think on me
- 228 O holy Lord, by all adored (PG)
- 350 We will walk through the valley
- 412 Bread of the world (Comm)
- 598 Show me your ways

Your choice....

- 635 Trust in the Lord
- 641 We are bound for the promised land
- 663 Be not afraid
- 673 Psalm 50 (51) (Resp Ps)
- *751 Hear us, almighty Lord (E/G)
- 770 My people, I hear you calling (E/G)
- *788 Praise to you, O Christ (Gosp Acc)
- 791 Safe in the shadow
- AK1,3; 20 (Resp Ps); *46 (Gosp Acc)

Lent 2 *Lord, it is wonderful for us to be here'*
Genesis 12:1–4; Ps 32(33); 2 Tim 1:8–10; MATTHEW 17:1–9

- 28 At the name of Jesus
- 35 Be thou my vision
- 73 Fight the good fight (CT/R)
- 120 Holy Father, God of might (CT/R)
- 134 Immortal, invisible (E/G)
- 428 Christ is the world's light (CT/R)
- 530 Leave your country and your people
- 570 O raise your eyes on high and see

Your choice....

- 670 One thing I ask (Psalm 26 (27))
- 737 Eye has not seen
- 739 Father, we come to you
- 748 God, your glory we have seen
- 768 Shine, Jesus, shine
- 815 We walk by faith
- AK 16(cf Resp Ps), *46

Lent 3 *A spring of water welling up to eternal life*
Exodus 17:3–7; Ps 94(95); Rom 5:1–2,5–8; JOHN 4:5–42 (or 5–15.19–26,39–42)
See note on page 21 on the Scrutiny Rite. A cross + indicates suitable items:

Water of Life (Eucharist section)
- 65 Draw nigh and take (Comm)
- 104 Guide me, O thou great redeemer
- 225 O living water
- 260 Praise, my soul, the King of heaven
- +383 Abba, abba Father
- +400 As earth that is dry
- 435 Come, let us sing out our joy (Ps 94/5)
- 457 Fear not, rejoice
- +557 My God, you fathom my heart
- 559 New life!
- 592 Rock of ages, cleft for me
- 597 Shepherd of souls
- +659 Yahweh, I know you are near
- 663 You shall cross the barren desert
- 679 Psalm 94/5 (Resp Ps)

Your choice....

- +696 Adoramus te
- +710 O Lord, hear my prayer
- +746 God is my great desire
- +758 In the land there is a hunger
- +774 Now in this banquet (+ alternative refrains)
- +778 O God, I seek you
- +780 O Lord, be not mindful
- 781 Centre of my life
- 783 O that today (Ps 94/5) = AK28
- +788 Praise to you, O Christ (Gospel Acc)
- +812 Unless a grain of wheat
- +Lord in your mercy (Intercession Refrain: Office Section)
- AK22, 28 (cf Resp Ps), 34, *46, +76, +77

35

Lent 4 *I am the light of the world*

I Sam 16:1,6–7,10–13; Ps 22(23); Eph 5:8–14; JOHN 9:1–41 (or 1.6–9,13–17,34–38)
See note on page 21 on the Scrutiny Rite. A cross + indicates suitable items; see also Sundays 3 and 5:

19 Amazing grace
43 Christ is our King
140 I saw the grass
190 Man of Galilee
208 Now come to me all you who seek (E/G) (see Tunefinder)
266 Praise we our God with joy (CT/R)
311 The King of love my shepherd is★
312 The Lord's my shepherd★
319 The Spirit of the Lord
340 Walk with me, O my Lord
405 Awake, awake, fling off the night (E/G)
514 I'll sing God's praises★
Your choice....

615 The Lord is my shepherd★
654 Whey he day?
664 The eyes of the blind (CT/R)
667 Psalm 22 (23) Resp. Ps
764 Jesus, Lord of life and love
+774 Now in this banquet (with alt. refrain 1) (Comm)
+777 O Christe Domine Jesu (+ Ps 23)★ (E/G, Comm)
813 We're forgiven
824 You are the King of glory (CT/R)
★ indicates versions of Psalm 22/23
AK13 (cf Resp Ps), ★46

Lent 5 *I am the resurrection and the life*

Ezekiel 37:12–14; Ps 129 (130); Romans 8:8–11; JOHN 11:1–45 (or 3–7,17–20,33–45)
See note on page 21 on the Scrutiny Rite. A cross + indicates suitable items; see also Sundays 3 and 4:

★81 From the deep I lift my voice (E/G)
128 I am the bread of life (Comm)
325 This day God gives me
386 Again the Lord's own day is here (E/G)
★466 From the depths of sin and sadness (E/ Pen.Rite)
501 I am the bread of life (Comm)
523 Jesus the Lord said 'I am the bread'
578 Our help is the name of the Lord (cf Resp Ps)
Your choice.... (E/G)

585 Praise the Lord! Ye heavens, adore him
604 Sing to the mountains
689 Psalm 129 (130) (Resp Ps)
750 Who calls my life again
★770 O Christe Domine Jesu (+ Ps 129) (E/G, Comm)
+812 Unless a grain (Comm, CT)
AK36 (cf Resp Ps), ★46

NOTE ON HOLY WEEK. Extra items are suggested from **The Great Week** (McCrimmons), indicated GW.

Palm Sunday *His state was divine; yet Christ Jesus did not cling to his equality with God*

(Palms Gospel: Matthew 21:1–11); Isaiah 50:4–7; Ps 21(22); Phil 2:6–11; MATTHEW 26:14–27:66 (or 27:11–54)

Before Procession
Hosanna (GW)

Procession of Palms
8 All glory, laud and honour
107 Hail redeemer, King divine
271 Ride on, ride on in majesty

Liturgy of the Word
Psalm and Gospel Acclamation (GW)
Psalm: AK12

Songs based on 2R (Phil 2:6–11):
418 By his wounds
522 Jesus, the Holy Lamb of God
727 Before the heaven and earth

Extra suggestions:
1. Take care over the choice of the Holy holy (Hosanna is a key word today), along with the other Eucharistic acclamations.
2. Sing a communion thanksgiving song and leave the church in silence after Mass.
Your choice....

Meditations on the Passion
206 My song is love unknown
247 O sacred head
324 They say I am wise
506 I met you at the cross
Father, if this cup (GW) (CT)

The Triumph of Christ
642 We cry Hosanna, Lord
770 Christ triumphant
824 You are the king of glory

The Paschal Triduum

As Sunday is the centre of the Christian week, Easter (or, rather, the Paschal Triduum) is the centre of the Christian year. In the three days from Maundy Thursday evening to Easter Sunday evening the Church recalls the passion, death and resurrection of Christ, and seeks to be one with him in this 'passover'.

This is a journey we all made at our baptism when in a sacramental (which does not mean 'unreal') way, we ourselves died and rose with Christ. If we were baptised as infants, we will have been unaware of this process, and so can use the Paschal Triduum as an opportunity to relive it, maybe for the first time with true consciousness of what it is.

There may be others in the parish who are only just about to undertake it. In the early centuries of the church, the celebration of Initiation (baptism, confirmation and first communion) at the Easter vigil was an overwhelming experience, as contemporary descriptions show. In our time we are privileged to witness a revival of this spirit and a renewed awareness of what it is to be a member of the church of Christ.

Maundy Thursday *Evening Mass of the Lord's Supper*
Exodus 12:1–8,11–14; Ps 115(116); I Cor 11:23–26; JOHN 13:1–15

Entrance/Gathering
185 Love is his word
309 The heavenly word, proceeding forth
358 Where is love and loving-kindness
    or God is love (GW)
653 When the time came

Liturgy of the Word
Psalm and Gospel Acclamation in GW
380 A new commandment (cf Gosp Acc)

Washing of Feet
327 This is my will
489 Greater love has no man
628 This is what Yahweh asks of you
    The Lord Jesus (GW)
    If I, your Lord and Master (GW)

Preparation of Gifts
    Ubi Caritas (GW)
139 Into one we all are gathered

Your choice....

Eucharistic Songs
 95 Draw nigh, and take
217 O Father, now the hour has come
249 O thou who at thy Eucharist
399 An upper room
403 As one body we are wed
408 Before Christ died
623 This is my body, broken for you
683 How can I repay the Lord (Ps114/115)
    Come, Christ's beloved (GW)
    Eat this bread (GW)
    AK68

The Procession
216 Of the glorious body telling
716 Pange lingua

After
    Stay with me (GW)

Good Friday *The Celebration of the Lord's Passion*
Isaiah 52:13–53:12; Ps 30(31); Heb 4:14–16; 5:7–9; JOHN 18:1–19:42

Liturgy of the Word
Psalm and Gospel Acc: GW
Intercession Responses (sing after 1st section of
each prayer)
- Divine Office section

Veneration of the Cross
(n.b. today's theme is the triumph of the Cross,
rather than personal devotion to the sufferings of
Christ)
    Reproaches: GW
279 Sing, my tongue, the glorious battle
316 There is a green hill far away
318 The royal banners forward go
347 Were you there when they crucified my Lord
355 When I survey the wondrous cross
419 By the cross which did to death

Communion Rite
    Jesus, remember me (GW)
262 Praise to the holiest in the height
730 Christ triumphant
Your choice....

The Easter Vigil *The Resurrection of the Lord*

Liturgy of Light
Lumen Christi; Exsultet GW

Liturgy of the Word
A full set of psalms and Alleluia: GW

In Celebration Hymnal:

Ps 103 (682)
538 Like the deer (Psalm 42)
552 Lumen Christi (Gospel Acclamation)
814 We shall draw water (Psalm after 5th reading)
Ps 50 (673)
Ps 117 (686)
AK20 (Ps 50)

Liturgy of Baptism
Water of life (Eucharist section)
227 O living water
244 O praise ye the Lord
400 As earth that is dry
420 Called to be servants
614 The light of Christ
621 There is one Lord
784 Oh healing river
826 You have put on Christ
AK77

The risen Christ
S3   Now the green blade riseth
27   At the Lamb's high feast
153 Jesus Christ is risen today
328 This joyful Eastertide
395 Alleluia, alleluia, give thanks to the risen Lord
627 This is the night
Your choice....

Easter Sunday *Peter saw the tomb and believed that Jesus had truly risen*
Acts 10:34,37–43; Ps 117(118); Col 3:1–4 or I Cor 5:6–8; JOHN 20:1–9
Sprinkling rite: Water of life (Eucharist section)
430 Christ our Lord has come to save his people

Other hymns as at Vigil, plus General Eastertide (below), especially:
Hail thee, festival day (GW)
27   At the Lamb's high feast
38   Bring, all ye dear-bought nations (sequence)
44   Christ the Lord is risen today (sequence)
423 Christ is arisen, alleluia
424 Christ is alive
431 Christ our pasch has been slain
486 Good Christian men
Your choice....

622 Thine be the glory
624/5 This is the day (E/G)
721 Victimae paschali (sequence)
736 Early morning (E/G)
*745 Free as is the morning sun
796 Surrexit Christus (Comm/CT/R)
*809 We have a gospel to proclaim
AK33 (cf Resp Ps)

39

EASTERTIDE: GENERAL

S3 Now the green blade	526 Keep in mind
27 At the Lamb's high feast	552 Lumen Christi (Gospel Acclamation)
31 Battle is o'er	604 Sing to the mountains
38 Bring, all ye dear-bought nations	621 There is one Lord
42 Christ is King of earth and heaven	622 Thine be the glory
97 God is love, his the care	624/5 This is the day
302 The day of resurrection	626 This is the feast of victory
307 The green life rises from the earth (Comm)	632 To be the body of the Lord
328 This joyful Eastertide	643 We form one Church, one Christian folk
344 We celebrate this festive day	686 Psalm 117(118)
363 Ye choirs of New Jerusalem	717 Regina caeli
384 Abba, Father, send your Spirit	735 Confitemini Domino (from Ps 117/118) (E/G, Comm)
423 Christ has arisen, alleluia!	745 Free as is the morning sun (CT/R)
424 Christ is alive, with joy we sing	748 God, your glory we have seen (CT/R)
430 Christ our Lord has come (Blessing of Water; E/G)	756 If God should lead us
431 Christ our Pasch has been slain (E/G)	762 Jesus is Lord!
433 Come God's people, sing for joy	796 Surrexit Christus (Comm/CT/R)
467 Gather Christians, let's now celebrate (E/G)	803 To God be the glory
486 Good Christian men, rejoice and sing!	809 We have a Gospel to proclaim
493 He is Lord	824 You are the King of glory
494 He is risen, alleluia! (Ps 99/100)	826 You have put on Christ (Blessing of Water; CT)
495 He is risen, tell the story	AK33, 47, 82
512 I will sing, I will sing	

Easter 2 *Thomas acknowledges the risen Jesus*
Acts 2:42–47; Ps 117(118); I Peter 1:3–9; JOHN 20:19–31

56 Crown him with many crowns (v3: Gosp)	735 Confitemini Domino (E/G, Comm)
95 Godhead here in hiding (v.4: Gosp)	756 If God should lead us
302 The day of resurrection	762 Jesus is Lord (CT/R)
364 Ye sons and daughters (vv.8–9)	815 We walk by faith
433 Come, God's people	AK47
493 He is Lord	
Your choice....	

Easter 3 *They recognised him in the breaking of bread*
Acts 2:14,22–33; Ps 15(16); I Peter 1:17–21; LUKE 24:13–35

344 We celebrate this festive day (E/G)	774 Now in this banquet
543 Lord, enthroned in heavenly splendour (CT/R)	775 O changeless Christ
571 O what a gift (see v.8)	781 O Lord, you are the centre (cf. Psalm)
605 Sing to the world (see v.3) (E/G)	787 Praise now your God
764 Jesus, Lord of life and love	802 Those who were in the dark
765 Jesus, you're the one = AK69	AK69
Your choice....	

Easter 4 *I am the gate of the sheepfold*
Acts 2:14,36–41; Ps 22(23); I Peter 2:20–25; JOHN 10:1–10

187 Loving shepherd of thy sheep	667 Psalm 22 (23)
266 Praise we our God with joy (CT/R)	731 Come, rejoice before your Maker (E/G)
311 The King of love my shepherd is	777 O Christe Domine Jesu (+ ps 23) (Comm)
312 The Lord's my shepherd	793 Sing, all creation (E/G)
523 Jesus the Lord said 'I am the bread'	795 Sing it in the valleys = AK84 (CT/R)
597 Shepherd of souls (Comm)	AK 13 (cf Resp Ps), 81, 84
615 The Lord is my shepherd	

Your choice....

Easter 5 *I am the Way, the Truth and the Life*
Acts 6:1–7; Ps 32(33); I Peter 2:4–9; JOHN 14:1–12

181 Lord of all hopefulness	598 Show me your ways
428 Christ is the world's light (v.1 cf Gosp)	628 This is what Yahweh asks
450 Father, I place into your hands	745 I received the living God (CT)
523 Jesus the Lord said	763 Jesus, lead the way (CT/R)
525 Jesus, you are Lord	825 You are the vine = AK67
579 Our Saviour Jesus Christ proclaimed	811 We have been told
581 Peace is my parting gift	AK67, 82
588 Rejoice and shout for joy (cf Psalm)	

Your choice....

Easter 6 *If you love me, keep my commandments*
Acts 8:5–8,14–17; Ps 65(66); I Peter 3:15–18; JOHN 14:23

7 Alleluia, sing to Jesus (v.2 cf Gosp)	548 Lord, this paschal time
32 Be still and know (cf Gospel)	604 Sing to the mountains
327 This is my will	623 This is my body (Comm)
391 All you nations (cf Psalm) (E/G)	724 Come we that love the Lord
417 But I say unto you	761 It is good to give thanks
420 Called to be servants	812 Unless a grain of wheat (v.5 cf Gospel)
502 I am the vine	(Comm)
525 Jesus, you are Lord	AK23 (cf Resp Ps)
526 Keep in mind	

Your choice....

The Ascension *Jesus at the right hand of God*
Acts 1:1–11; Ps 46(47); Eph 1:17–23; MATTHEW 28:16–20

7	Alleluia, sing to Jesus	525	Jesus, you are Lord
28	At the name of Jesus	703	Go out to the whole world (round)
108	Hail the day that sees him rise	708	Let us go forth (round)
207	New praises be given	714	Stand and stare not (round) (CT)
270	Rejoice! the Lord is King!	727	Before the heaven and earth
308	The head that once was crowned	730	Christ triumphant
429	Christ is the world's redeemer (see Tunefinder)	748	God, your glory we have seen (CT/R)
493	He is Lord	762	Jesus is Lord
510	I will be with you		AK19 (cf Resp Ps)

Your choice....

Easter 7 *Father, the hour has come: glorify your Son, so that your Son may glorify you*
Acts 1:12–14; Ps 26(27); I Peter 4:13–16; JOHN 17:1–11
Hymns for Ascension, also:

42	Christ is King of earth and heaven	670	Psalm 26(27): Resp. Psalm
118	He was born like you and I	748	God, your glory we have seen (CT/R)
217	O Father, now the hour has come (see Tunefinder)	762	Jesus is Lord
543	Lord, enthroned in heavenly splendour (CT/R)	769	Majesty
617	The Spirit is moving	803	To God be the glory (CT/R)
618	The Spirit lives to set us free	812	Unless a grain of wheat (Comm)
			AK16 (cf Resp Ps)

Your choice....

Pentecost *Send forth your Spirit, O Lord*
Acts 2:1–11; Ps 103(104); I Cor 12:3–7,12–13; JOHN 20:19–23

49	Come down, O love divine	638	Veni, sancte Spiritus (E/G)
50	Come, holy Ghost	657	Wind and fire
124	Holy Spirit, Lord of light (Sequence)	682	Psalm 103(104): Resp. Psalm
125	Holy Spirit of fire	700	Breath of life (round)
225	Oh living water	720	Veni creator Spiritus (E/G)
289	Spirit of the living God	744	Forth in the peace of Christ (CT/R)
595/6	Send forth your Spirit	797	The gift of the Holy Spirit (CT/R)
617	The Spirit is moving		AK32 (cf Resp Ps); 44 (Gosp Acc)
625	This is the day		

Your choice....

Trinity *A God of tenderness, who made us and redeemed us*

Exodus 34:4–6,8–9; Daniel 3:52–56; 2 Cor 13:11–13; JOHN 3:16–18

70 Father most holy (E/G)	452 Father, in my life
121 Holy God, we praise thy name (E/G)	453 Father, Lord of all creation (CT/R)
122/3 Holy, holy, holy (E/G)	455 Father, we praise you, now the night is over (E/G)
130 I believe in God the Father	
165 Lead us, heavenly Father	459 Firm is our faith
194 Merrily on	702 Glory be to God the Father (round)
198 Most ancient of all mysteries	740 For call to faith
284 Sing praises to the living God	768 Lord, the light of your love
451 Father in heaven	AK85

Your choice....

The Body and Blood of Christ (Corpus Christi)

Anyone who eats this bread will live for ever

Deut 8:2–3,14–16; Ps 147; I Cor 10:16–17; JOHN 6:51–58

65 Draw nigh and take (Comm)	543 Lord enthroned in heavenly splendour (CT/R)
74 Fill my house	567 O food of travellers
128 I am the bread of life (see also 501)	597 Shepherd of souls
249 O thou who at thy Eucharist (CT/R)	623 This is my body
264 Praise to the Lord, the Almighty (PG)	648 Welcome, all ye noble saints (PG)
324 They say I am wise	653 When the time came (E/G)
399 An upper room	764 Jesus, Lord of life and love
403 As one body (Comm)	765 Jesus, you're the one I love = AK69
408 Before Christ died (see Tunefinder)	774 Now in this banquet (Comm)
412 Bread of the world (for choir?)	787 Praise now your God (CT/R)
438 Come, O Lord, to my heart	802 Those who were in the dark (CT/R)
501 I am the bread of life	Eucharist Section: Lamb of God 2–4
521 Jesus said 'I am the bread'	AK51, 66, 68, 69
523 Jesus the Lord said 'I am the bread'	

Your choice....

Sacred Heart *God is love*

Deut 7:6–11; Ps 102 (103); I John 4:7–16; MATTHEW 11:25–30

15 All ye who seek a comfort sure	388 All for Jesus
96 God is love	404 As the bridegroom
97 God is love, his the care	415 Bright star of morning
150 Jesu, lover of my soul	471 Give us the will to listen
161 King of glory, King of peace	499 His light now shines
248 O Sacred Heart	592 Rock of ages
260 Praise, my soul (cf Resp Ps)	696 Adoramus te, Domine
288 Soul of my Saviour	728 Bless the Lord, my soul (cf Resp Ps)
293 Sweet heart of Jesus	765 Jesus, you're the one I love = AK 69
333 To Christ, the Prince of peace	777 O Christe Domine Jesu
334 To Jesus' heart all-burning	AK31 (cf Resp Ps), 69, 76, 77

Your choice...

Year A: Ordinary Time

It is in Ordinary Time that one can see best the importance of the Christian Sunday. 'No particular aspect of the mystery of Christ is celebrated in Ordinary Time,' says the *Roman Calendar* (43); instead, Christ in all his fullness is celebrated: *Again the Lord's own day is here* (see hymn 386). God, says the Book of Genesis, rested on the seventh day (hence the Sabbath.) Christ rose from the dead 'on the first day of the week' and so Sunday has become the Lord's Day, on which every week Christians celebrate the Lord's 'paschal mystery'. In Ordinary Time the Sundays are characterised by the semi-continuous reading of a particular Gospel, spread over the year, so that we hear about Jesus' teaching, miracles and ministry and give thanks for them.

Year A is the Year of Matthew, as has already been said. Matthew's Gospel was written, it is thought, for Jewish Christians, as it contains frequent demonstrations of how Jesus fulfils the promises made to Israel (see Advent 4, Christmas Vigil, Epiphany, Sundays 3, 6, and 27 in Ordinary Time, etc). Conversely, the scribes and pharisees, who thought that they were the keepers of Israel's heritage, are shown to have been superseded by the new Israel, the Church. At the beginning of Matthew we hear of 'Emmanuel, God with us' and at the very end Jesus says 'I am with you always, even to the end of time'.

The Gospel is organised around five 'sermons' of which the Sermon on the Mount is the best known. Each one has a section of narrative preceding it, like this: *

    I. Life in the Kingdom
      Narrative: the call of the Disciples (Sunday 3)
      Sermon: The Sermon on the Mount (Suns 4–9)
    II. The Spread of the Kingdom
      Narrative: The call of Levi (10)
      Sermon: The Mission Sermon (11–13)
    III. The Mystery of the Kingdom
      Narrative: The revelation to the simple (14)
      Sermon: The Parable Sermon (15–17)
    IV. God's Kingdom on earth – the Church of Christ
      Narrative: Three miracles; Peter's confession of faith
    (18–22)

    V. The end of Christ's ministry: who will enter the
    Kingdom?
      Narrative: Parables and incidents (25–31)
      Sermon: The final sermon (32–3)
    Conclusion: God's Kingdom fulfilled (34, Christ the King)

 See Guide to the Lectionary, Fr John Fitzsimmons, pp86, 88–9)

NOTES

1. Asterisked hymns may be used on more than one Sunday in a particular season.
2. Some hymns are based on one or other of the Readings of the day and these are noted as follows: 1R = First Reading; 2R = Second Reading; Gosp = Gospel;

3. Suggestions for the use of the hymns at Mass are noted thus (note that these are *suggestions* only): E/G = Entrance/Gathering; PG = Preparation of Gifts; Comm = Communion; R = Recessional, CT/R = Communion Thanksgiving or Recessional.

4. If you need EXTRA HYMNS: see p.27

5. Learning NEW HYMNS: see p.24

6. Space is provided after each Sunday for your own choice of hymns. Good ideas should be written down straight away so they are not forgotten.

Sunday 2 *Look, there is the Lamb of God.*
Isaiah 49:3,56; Ps 39(40); I Cor 1:1–3; JOHN 1:29–34

14 All this world belongs to Jesus	629 Thou whose almighty Word (E/G)
28 At the name of Jesus	740 For call to faith
319 The Spirit of the Lord	744 Forth in the peace of Christ
426 Christ is coming	747 God who spoke in the beginning (see Tunefinder)
428 Christ is the world's light (CT/R)	782 O most high and glorious God (CT/R)
430 Christ our Lord has come to save (Blessing of Water, E/G)	802 Behold the Lamb of God
482 God most high of all creation	816 What do you want of me, Lord
500 Our God reigns	822 You are the Lord
508 Here I am, Lord	AK18 (cf Resp Ps), 76
518 In the beginning	Additional suggestion: use Lamb of God 2,3, or 4 (Eucharist)
619 The Spirit of God rests upon me	

Your choice....

Sunday 3 *The people that lived in darkness have seen a great light*
Isaiah 8:23–9:3; Ps 26(27); I Cor 1:10–13,17; MATTHEW 4:12–23 (or 12–17)

43 Christ is our king	545 Lord, in everything I do (PG)
45 Colours of day	550 Lord, you have come to the lakeside
60 Dear Lord and Father	598 Show me your ways
99 Go tell everyone (CT/R)	605 Sing to the world (CT/R)
242 Open your ears O Christian people	614 The light of Christ (E/G)
310 The King of glory comes (E/G)	650 What would you ask of me
315 The race that long in darkness pined (E/G)	670 Psalm 26(27): Resp Psalm
428 Christ is the world's light	724 All the ends of the earth
446 Each morning with its newborn light (see Tunefinder)	752 Here in this place (E/G)
460 Follow me	768 Lord, the light of your love (CT/R)
482 God most high of all creation	792 Sing a new song (E/G)
496 He's a most unusual man	802 Behold the lamb of God
499 His light now shines	823 You shall go out with joy
	AK16 (cf Resp Ps)

Your choice....

Sunday 4 *Blessed are the poor in spirit...*

Zeph 2:3; 3:12–13; Ps 145; I Cor 1:26–31; MATTHEW 5:1–12

A Mass for Peace and Justice may be celebrated today – for hymns, see p.101

36	Blest are the pure in heart	345	We gather together (v.3 cf 2R) (E/G)
37	Breathe on me, breath of God]	583	Peacetime
79	Forth in thy name, O Lord, I go (CT/R)	612	The Church is wherever
111	Happy the man who wanders with the Lord	699	The Beatitudes
119	He who would valiant be	726	As a tree planted
208	Now come to me all you who seek (see Tunefinder)	760	In your love remember me
		799	The master came (CT/R)
320	The Kingdom = AK73	817	What does the Lord require
256	Peacemakers		AK39 (cf Resp Ps), 73

Your choice....

Sunday 5 *Seeing your good works, they may give praise to your Father*

Isaiah 58:7–10; Ps 111(112); I Cor 2:1–5; MATTHEW 5:13–16

51	Come, Lord Jesus, come	449	Father, hear the prayer we offer
78/744	Forth in the peace of Christ (CT/R)	593	Seek ye first
102	Go, the Mass is ended	612	The Church is wherever
119	He who would valiant be	797	The gift of the Holy Spirit
254	Peace is flowing like a river	798	The Kingdom of God
296	Take my hands	807	We are your people
313	The Mass is ended (R)	817	What does the Lord require
417	But I say unto you		

Your choice....

Sunday 6 *They are happy who follow God's law*

Ecclus 15:15–20; Ps 118(119); I Cor 2:6–10; MATTHEW 5:17–37 (or 20–22,27–28,33–34,37)

36	Blest are the pure in heart	549	Lord, thy word abideth
111	Happy the man who wanders with the Lord	598	Show me your ways
178	Lord, for tomorrow and its needs	608	Take my life and let it be (PG)
201	My God, accept my heart	666	Psalm 18(19)
223	O God, thy people gather (see Tunefinder) (E/G)	743	Forgive our sins as we forgive
		782	O most high and glorious God
228	Oh holy Lord, by all adored (PG)	799	The master came to give good news (CT/R)
342	We are one in the Spirit (CT/R)	801	The word of God = AK11
547	Lord of creation (PG)		AK11

Your choice....

Sunday 7 *You have learnt how it was said... But I say to you...*
Lev 19:1–2,17–18; Ps 102(103); I Cor 3:16–23; MATTHEW 5:38–48

76	Follow Christ and love the world	497	Help us accept each other
136	In Christ there is no east or west	578	Our help is the name (cf Resp Ps) (E/G)
139	Into one we all are gathered	636	Unite us, Lord, in peace (Comm)
189	Make me a channel of your peace	681	Psalm 102 (103) (Resp Ps)
210	Now Jesus said	728	Bless the Lord my soul (cf. Resp Ps)
226	Oh Lord, all the world	750	Who calls my life (cf Resp Ps)
260	Praise my soul the King of heaven (cf Resp Ps)	786	Peace I give
		797	The gift of the Holy Spirit (CT/R)
327	This is my will	799	The master came (CT/R)
358	Where is love and loving-kindness	807	We are your people
380	A new commandment	817	What does the Lord require
417	But I say unto you	AK31 (cf Resp Ps), 83	

Your choice....

Sunday 8 *Do not worry about tomorrow*
Isaiah 49:14–15; Ps 61(62); I Cor 4:1–5; MATTHEW 6:24–34

63	Do not worry over what to eat	558	My soul is longing for your peace
73	Fight the good fight	593	Seek ye first
74	Fill my house unto the fullest	630	Though the mountains may fall (1R)
104	Guide me, O thou great Redeemer	635	Trust in the Lord
164	Lead kindly light	746	God is my great desire
296	Take my hands	758	In the land there is a hunger
362	Yahweh, you are my strength	759	In the Lord
402	As long as men on earth	761	It is good to give thanks
450	Father, I place into your hands	765	Jesus you're the one = AK69
481	God made the birds	781	O God, you are the centre
511	I will never forget you (1R)	AK10, 26, 69	
517	In God alone is there rest		

Your choice....

Sunday 9 *A house built on rock*
Deut 11:18,26–28,32; Ps 30(31); Rom 3:21–25,28; MATTHEW 7:21–27

s1	God gives his people strength	447	Faith in God can move the mountains
6	Alleluia! I will praise the Father	578	Our help is the name of the Lord (E/G)
35	Be thou my vision	592	Rock of ages
41	Christ be beside me	635	Trust in the Lord
150	Jesu, lover of my soul	794	Sing of the Lord's goodness
208	Now come to me all you who seek (E/G)	795	Sing it in the valleys = AK84
222	O God our help in ages past	811	We have been told
325	This day God gives me	825	You are the vine = AK67
389	All my hope on God is founded	AL67, 84	
435	Come, let us sing out our joy (E/G)		

Your choice....

Sunday 10 *I did not come to call the virtuous, but sinners*

Hosea 6:3–6; Ps 49(50); Rom 4:18–25; MATTHEW 9:9–13

51 Come, Lord Jesus, come	643 We form one Church (v3 cf Gosp)
60 Dear Lord and Father of mankind	770 My people, I hear you calling
161 King of glory, king of peace	798 The Kingdom of God
506 I met you at the cross	799 The Master came (CT/R)
508 I, the Lord of sea and sky	803 To God be the glory (CT/R)
591 Return to the Lord (E/G)	813 We're forgiven
597 Shepherd of souls (Comm)	816 What do you want of me, Lord?

Your choice....

Sunday 11 *He made us, we belong to him*

Exodus 19:2–6; Ps 99(100); Rom 5:6–11; MATTHEW 9:36–10:8

★ indicates versions of Ps 99(100), the Responsorial Psalm

★10 All people that on earth do dwell (E/G)	547 Lord of creation (PG)
45 Colours of day	612 The Church is wherever
78/744 Forth in the peace of Christ (CT/R)	680 Psalm 99(100) = Resp. Psalm
99 God's spirit is in my heart (CT/R)	703 Go out to the whole world (round)
102 Go, the Mass is ended	★731 Come, rejoice (E/G)
268 Reap me the earth (PG)	744 see 78
296 Take my hands (PG)	748 God, your glory we have seen (CT/R)
★390 All the earth proclaim the Lord (E/G)	★793 Sing, all creation (E/G)
478 God gives us harvest (PG)	809 We have a gospel to proclaim (CT/R)
510 I will be with you (CT/R)	AK30 (cf Resp Ps)
530 Leave your country	

Your choice....

Sunday 12 *Do not be afraid of those who kill the body but cannot kill the soul*

Jeremiah 20:10–13; Ps 68(69); Rom 5:12–15; MATTHEW 10:26–33

119 He who would valiant be	656 Who wants to live as God here on this earth
340 Walk with me, O my Lord	663 You shall cross the barren desert
379 A mighty stronghold is our God	710 O Lord hear my prayer
444 Do not be afraid	763 Jesus, lead the way
449 Father, hear the prayer we offer	765 Jesus, you're the one = AK69
452 Father, in my life I see	771 Nothing can ever take away
471 Give us the will to listen	791 Safe in the shadow
515 If God is for us	802 Those who were in the dark
556 My God, my God, don't ever desert me	806 Be here among us (CT/R)
644 We gather together to ask the Lord's blessing (E/G)	AK69

Your choice....

Sunday 13 *Anyone who welcomes my disciple, welcomes me*
2 Kings 4:8–11,14–16; Ps 88(89); Rom 6:3–4,8–11; MATTHEW 10:37–42

Water of life (Blessing of Water: cf 2R)

64	Do you know that the Lord walks on earth?
73	Fight the good fight
201	My God, accept my heart
352	Whatsoever you do
353	When I needed a neighbour
399	An upper room (comm)
530	Leave your country and your people
540	Look around you
545	Lord, in everything I do

574	Oh the word of my Lord
656	Who wants to live as God
706/7	Jubilate Deo
709	Misericordias Domini (cf Resp Psalm)
730	Christ triumphant
746	God is my great desire
781	O Lord, you are the centre
812	Unless a grain of wheat
826	You have put on Christ (Blessing of Water: cf 2R)

Your choice....

Sunday 14 *Come to me all you who labour... I am gentle and humble of heart*
Zech 9:9–10; Ps 144(145); Rom 8:9,11–13; MATTHEW 11:25–30

15	All ye who seek a comfort sure
150	Jesu, lover of my soul
151	Jesu, meek and lowly
154	Jesu, gentlest Saviour
159	Just a closer walk with thee
208	Now come to me all you who seek (see Tunefinder) (E/G)
231	Oh the love of my Lord is the essence
278	Sing my soul
428	Christ is the world's light (v1 cf Gosp)
545	Lord, in everything I do (PG)
579	Our Saviour Jesus Christ proclaimed
581	Peace is my parting gift (vv 3–4 cf Gosp)

608	Take my life and let it be (PG)
612	The Church is wherever
642	We cry 'Hosanna,' Lord (1R)
647	We thank you, Father
691	Ps 144 (145) (Resp Ps)
734	Come we that love the Lord
748	God, your glory we have seen
761	It is good to give thanks
794	Sing of the Lord's goodness
804	To Jesus Christ, our sovereign King (CT/R)
810	We have a King who comes in glory
AK38	(cf Resp Ps)

Your choice....

.

Sunday 15 *The Word that I speak does not return to me empty*
Isaiah 55:10–11; Ps 64(65); Rom 8:18–23; MATTHEW 13:1–23 (or 1–9)

Water of life (Eucharist section: Blessing of Water)

138	In the earth the small seed
172	Light of our darkness, word of God
273	Seasons come, seasons go
329	This little light of mine
400	As earth that is dry (1R)
402	As long as men on earth
461	For the fruits of his creation (PG)
478	God gives us harvest (PG)
502	I am the vine
616	The seed is Christ's
618	The Spirit lives to set us free (2R)
637	Upon this table, Lord (PG)

726	As a tree planted
729	Christ's church shall glory
737	Eye has not seen (2R)
748	God, your glory
758	In the land there is a hunger
775	O changeless Christ
806	Be here among us
811	We have been told
812	Unless a grain
825	You are the vine = AK67
AK67	

Your choice....

Sunday 16 *O Lord, slow to anger, abounding in love*
Wisdom 12:13,16–19; Ps 85(86); Rom 8:26–27; MATTHEW 13:24–43 (or 24–30)

19	Amazing grace!	560	No one can give to me that peace
221	O God of earth and altar (E/G)	563	Now watch for God's coming (Gosp)
223	O God, thy people gather (E/G)	616	The seed is Christ's
304	The farmer in the fertile field	644	We gather together (E/G)
338	Vaster far than any ocean	656	Who wants to live as God
410	Blest are you, Lord God (PG)	660	You, Israel, return now (E/G)
424	Christ is alive (CT/R)	728	Bless the Lord, my soul (E/G)
461	For the fruits (if harvest time)	750	Who calls my life again
480	God is working his purpose out	758	God, your glory we have seen
485	God's spirit precedes us (2R)	798	The kingdom of God
488	Grant us thy peace	806	Be here among us (CT/R)

Your choice....

Sunday 17 *Choose the real treasure*
I Kings 3:5,7–12; Ps 118(119); Rom 8:28–30; MATTHEW 13:44–52 (or 44–46)

35	Be thou my vision	598	Show me your ways
41	Christ be beside me	608	Take my life (PG)
63	Do not worry over what to eat	634	Together we journey
152	Jesu, the very thought of thee	650	What would you ask of me
181	Lord of all hopefulness	760	In your love remember me = AK15
296	Take my hands (PG)	798	The kingdom of God
388	All for Jesus	799	The master came to give good news (CT/R)
397	Almighty Father, who for us	801	The word of God = AK11
463	For to those who love God (2R)		AK11, 15

Your choice....

Sunday 18 *A God who feeds us*
Isaiah 55:1–3; Ps 144(145); Rom 8:35,37–39; MATTHEW 14:13–21

7	Alleluia! sing to Jesus	567	O food of travellers
65	Draw nigh and take (Comm)	597	Shepherd of souls
85	Give me yourself	643	We form one Church
128	I am the bread of life	690	Ps 135
166	Let all mortal flesh (PG)	691	Ps 144 (145) (Resp Ps)
202	My God, and is thy table spread	754	I received the living God (CT)
400	As earth that is dry (1R)	765	Jesus, you're the one I love = AK69
402	As long as men on earth are living	774	Nothing can ever take away (2R)
402	As one body (Comm)	774	Now in this banquet
410	Blest are you, Lord God (PG)	785	One shall tell another
440	Day and night the heavens	787	Praise now your God
462	For to those who love God (2R)	802	Those who were in the dark
469	Gifts of bread and wine (PG)	814	We shall draw water joyfully (1R)
515	If God is for us (2R)	821	With open hands (PG)
516	If God is our defender (2R)		AK38 (cf Resp Ps), 69

Your choice....

Sunday 19 *Give us your saving help. Calm the sea*

I Kings 19:9,11–13; Ps 84(85); Rom 9:1–5; MATTHEW 14:22–23

28	At the name of Jesus	456	Fear not, for I have redeemed you
33	Be still and know	510	I will be with you (CT/R)
60	Dear Lord and Father (v5: 1R)	553	May the peace of the Lord
67	Eternal Father, strong to save	560	No-one can give to me
117	He's got the whole world	582	Peace, perfect peace in this dark world
156	Jesus is God!	663	You shall cross the barren desert(CT/R)
165	Lead us, heavenly Father	676	Ps 84 (85) (Resp Ps)
222	O God, our help in ages past	739	Father, we come to you (E/G)
253	O worship the King (E/G)	763	Jesus, lead the way
294	Sweet sacrament divine (Comm)	775	O changeless Christ
340	Walk with me, O my Lord	781	Centre of my life
359	Where would we be without Christ	791	Safe in the shadow
407	Be still, my soul	795	Sing it in the valleys = AK84
444	Do not be afraid	822	You are the Lord
447	Faith in God can move the mountains		AK25 (cf Resp Ps), 84

Your choice....

Sunday 20 *My house is a house of prayer for all peoples*

Isaiah 56:1,6–7; Ps 66(67); Rom 11:13–15,29–32; MATTHEW 15:21–28

10	All people that on earth do dwell (E/G)	633	To God our Father (see Tunefinder)
53	Come praise the Lord, the Almighty (PG)	724	All the ends of the earth (E/G)
78/744	Forth in the name (CT/R)	744	see 78
391	All you nations (E/G)	772	New songs of celebration
395	Alleluia, give thanks	792	Sing a new song (E/G)
427	Christ is made the sure foundation (E/G)	818	What is this place (E/G)
523	Jesus the Lord said 'I am the bread' (Comm)	820	When the King shall come (CT/R)
605	Sing to the world of Christ (CT/R)	822	You are the Lord (CT/R)
614	The light of Christ	824	You are the King of glory (CT/R)

Your choice....

Sunday 21 *On this rock I will build my church*

Isaiah 22:19–23; Ps 137(138); Rom 11:33–36; MATTHEW 16:13–20

75	Firmly I believe and truly	550	Lord, you have come to the lakeside
130	I believe in God the Father	612	The Church is wherever
156	Jesus is God!	643	We form one Church
167	Let all that is within me	655	Who is she that stands triumphant
300	The Church's one foundation	729	Christ's church shall glory
331	Thy hand, O God, has guided	747	God who spoke in the beginning
389	All my hope on God is founded (E/G)	762	Jesus is Lord!
427	Christ is made the sure foundation (E/G)	804	To Jesus Christ our Sovereign King
458	Feed my lambs	815	We walk by faith
459	Firm is our faith	827	We believe
493	He is Lord		AK37 (cf Resp Ps)

Your choice....

Sunday 22 *Anyone who loses his life for my sake will find it*

Jer 20:7–9; Ps 62(63); Rom 12:1–2; MATTHEW 16:21–27

35	Be thou my vision	522	Jesus the holy Lamb of God
36	Blest are the pure in heart	530	Leave your country
73	Fight the good fight	545	Lord, in everything I do
79	Forth in thy name, O Lord	598	Show me your ways
119	He who would valiant be	656	Who wants to live as God
201	My God, accept my heart	674	Ps 62 (63) (Resp Ps)
296	Take my hands	707	Jubilate Deo (E/G)
313	The Mass is ended	727	Before the heaven and earth
316	There is a green hill far away	730	Christ triumphant
355	When I survey	746	God is my great desire
418	By his wounds	773	Nothing can ever take away
441	Day by day	778	Oh God I seek you (cf Resp Ps)
449	Father, hear the prayer we offer	798	The Kingdom of God
460	Follow me	812	Unless a grain of wheat (Comm/CT)
519	It's a long hard journey	AK22	cf Resp Ps

Your choice....

Sunday 23 *Our duty to win people back to the right path*

Ezekiel 33:7–9; Ps 94(95); Rom 13:8–10; MATTHEW 18:15–20

s7	Lord, make me an instrument of your peace	579	Our Saviour Jesus Christ (v1 cf Gosp)
76	Follow Christ and love the world	591	Return to the Lord (E/G)
139	Into one we all are gathered	612	The Church is wherever
170	Let's make peace in our hearts	623	This is my body (Comm)
189	Make me a channel	634	Together we journey
223	O God, thy people gather (E/G) (see Tunefinder)	660	You, Israel, return now
		679	Ps 94 (95)(Resp Ps)
342	We are one in the Spirit	743	Forgive us, Lord, as we forgive
358	Where is love and loving kindness	767	Lead us from death to life
435	Come, let us sing out (cf Resp Ps) (E/G)	780	O Lord, be not mindful (Pen.Rite)
453	Father, Lord of all creation	783	O that today (cf Resp Ps) = AK28
462	For the healing of the nations	798	The Kingdom of God
497	Help us accept each other	799	The master came (E/G)
532	Let all who share (R)	AK28	(cf Resp Ps)

Your choice....

Sunday 24 *God does not repay us according to our faults; neither should we*

Ecclus 27:30–28:7; Ps 102(103); Rom 14:7–9; MATTHEW 18:21–35

Some of last Sunday's hymns may be useful; also:

191	Many times I have turned	593	Seek ye first
226	Oh Lord, all the world	681	Ps 102 (103) (Resp Ps)
260	Praise, my soul (cf Resp Ps)	728	Bless the Lord, my soul (cf Resp Ps)
371	There is a world	743	Forgive our sins as we forgive
352	Whatsoever you do	750	Who calls my life (cf Resp Ps)
397	Almighty Father, who for us	770	My people, I hear you calling (E/G)
417	But I say unto you	776	O Christ the healer
477	God forgave my sin in Jesus' name	785	One shall tell another
489	Greater love has no man	797	The gift of the holy Spirit (CT/R)
497	Help us accept each other	799	The master came (CT/R)
578	Our help is the name of the Lord (cf Resp Ps)	807	We are your people

817 What does the Lord require   AK31 (cf Resp Ps)
Your choice....

Sunday 25   *God is close to those who call: but he rewards us as he decides*
Isaiah 55:6–9; Ps 144(145); Phil 1:2–24,27; MATTHEW 20:1–6

97	God is love: his the care	609	Tell out, my soul (CT/R)
134	Immortal, invisible	691	Ps 144 (145) (cf Resp Ps)
135	In bread we bring you	728	Bless the Lord
146	I will give you glory	761	It is good to give thanks (E/G)
171	Let us with a gladsome mind	785	One shall tell another
351	What can we offer you	798	The kingdom of God (CT/R)
402	As long as men on earth	810	We have a king who comes
547	Lord of creation (PG)		AK38 (cf Resp Ps)

Your choice....

Sunday 26   *He shows the path to those who stray*
Ezekiel 18:25–28; Ps 24(25); Phil 2:1–11 (or 1–5): MATTHEW 21:28–32

s1	God gives his people strength	578	Our help is the name of the Lord (E/G)
19	Amazing grace	648	Welcome, all ye noble saints
36	Blest are the pure heart	669	Ps 24 (25) (cf Resp Ps)
150	Jesu, lover of my soul	727	Before the heaven and earth (2R)
191	Many times I have turned	748	God, your glory we have seen (CT/R)
330	Thou wilt keep him	751	Hear us, almighty Lord (E/G)
338	Vaster far than any ocean	760	In your love remember me (cf Resp Ps) = AK15
477	God forgave my sin		
522	Jesus the holy Lamb of God (2R)	764	Jesus, Lord of life and love
542	Lord, confronted with your might	771	My soul cannot be still = AK5
544	Lord graciously hear us	780	O Lord, be not mindful (Pen.Rite)
577	Our Father, we have wandered (E/G)		AK5, 15

Your choice....

Sunday 27   *The vineyard of the Lord*
Isaiah 5:1–7; Ps 79(80); Phil 4:6–9; MATTHEW 21:33–43

55	Come, ye thankful people, come	591	Return to the Lord
88	Glory be to Jesus	632	To be the body of the Lord
138	In the earth the small seed	653	When the time came
206	My song is love unknown = AK80	730	Christ triumphant
268	Reap me the earth	745	Free as is the morning Sun (CT/R)
418	Christ suffered for you	762	Jesus is Lord!
429	Christ is the world's redeemer (see Tunefinder)	771	My soul cannot be still (E/G)
		803	To God be the glory (CT/R)
442	Dear love of my heart	809	We have a gospel to proclaim (CT/R)
478	God gives us harvest (PG)	825	You are the vine = AK67
508	Here I am, Lord		AK51, 67, 70, 79, 80

Sunday 28 *The wedding feast of the Lord*
Isaiah 25:6–10; Ps 22(23); Phil 4:12–14,19–20; MATTHEW 22:1–14 (or 1–10)

69	Father and lifegiver	615	The Lord is my shepherd (cf Resp Ps)
297	Take our bread, we ask you (PG)	648	Welcome, all ye noble saints (Comm)
300	The Church's one foundation	667	Ps 22 (23) (Resp Ps)
311	The King of love (cf Resp Ps)	670	One thing I ask (Comm/CT)
312	The Lord's my shepherd (cf Resp Ps)	752	Here in this place (E/G)
341	We are gathering together	774	Now in this banquet (Comm/CT)
344	We celebrate this festive day (E/G)	777	O Christe Domine Jesu (Comm/CT)
390	All the earth proclaim the Lord (E/G)	779	Oh how lovely is your dwelling place
438	Come, O Lord, to my heart (Comm)	785	One shall tell another
457	Fear not, rejoice and be glad	787	Praise now your God (CT/R)
501	I am the bread of life (Comm)	798	The kingdom of God
514	I'll sing God's praises (cf Resp Ps)	818	What is this place (E/G)
559	New life!	822	You are the Lord
563	Now watch for God's coming (E/G)	AK13 (cf Resp Ps), 16	
576	One day will come		

Your choice....

Sunday 29 *There is no other God besides me*
Isaiah 45:1,4–6; Ps 95(96); I Thess 1:1–5; MATTHEW 22:15–21

10	All people that on earth (E/G)	525	Jesus, you are Lord
28	At the name of Jesus	585	Praise the Lord! ye heavens
35	Be thou my vision	652	When morning gilds the skies
42	Christ is King of earth and heaven	768	Shine, Jesus, shine
86	Glorious God, king of creation	769	Majesty
121	Holy God, we praise thy name	792	Sing a new song
123	Holy, holy, holy	793	Sing, all creation
181	Immortal, invisible	794	Sing of the Lord's goodness
283	Sing praises to God	824	You are the King of glory
428	Christ is the world's light	AK66, 83	
493	He is Lord		

Your choice....

Sunday 30 *The greatest commandment of all*
Exodus 22:20–26; Ps 17(18); I Thess 1:5–10; MATTHEW 22:34–40

122	Holy holy	497	Help us accept each other
136	In Christ there is no east or west	623	This is my body (Comm)
139	Into one we all are gathered	628	This is what Yahweh asks
157	Jesus my Lord, my God	658	Would you like to be happy?
161	King of glory, king of peace	761	It is good to give thanks
185	Love is his word (esp v.6)	767	Lead us from death to life
204	My God I love thee	778	Oh God I seek you
327	This is my will, my one command	799	The master came to bring good news
358	Where are love and loving-kindness	807	We are your people
380	A new commandment	AK10 (cf Resp Ps), 83	
404	As the bridegroom to his chosen		

Your choice....

Sunday 31 *The greatest among you must be your servant*
Malachi 1:14–2:2,8–10; Ps 130(131); I Thess 2:7–9,13; MATTHEW 23:1–12

60 Dear Lord and Father of mankind
142 I sing the Lord God's praises (see Tunefinder)
221 O God of earth and altar (E/G)
237 O my Lord, within my heart
397 Almighty Father
479 God has gladdened my heart
488 Grant us thy peace
517 In God alone is there rest for my soul

558 My soul is longing (cf Resp Ps)
599 Sing a simple song
628 This is what Yahweh asks
636 Unite us, Lord, in peace
726 As a tree planted
727 Before the heaven and earth
760 In your love remember me = AK15
817 What does the Lord require
AK15

Your choice....

Sunday 32 *Watch and wait*
Wisdom 6:12–16; Ps 62(63); I Thess 4:13–18 (or 13–14); MATTHEW 25:1–13

35 Be thou my vision
141 I sing a song to you, Lord
158 Jesus! thou art coming
184 Love divine, all loves excelling
233 O Jesus Christ, remember
267 Promised Lord and Christ is he (CT/R)
350 We will walk through the valley
405 Awake, awake! fling off the night (E/G)
500 Our God reigns (CT/R)
504/505 I lift (up) my eyes
563 Now watch for God's coming
639 Wake, awake! for night is dying

640 Wake up! the dawn is near
674 Ps 62 (63) Resp Ps
746 God is my great desire
758 In the land there is a hunger
759 In the Lord I'll be ever thankful (E/G)
778 Your love is finer (cf Resp Ps)
805 Wait for the Lord (E/G)
806 Be here among us
810 We have a king
823 You shall go out with joy (CT/R)
AK32 (cf Resp Ps)

Your choice....

Sunday 33 *Well done, good and faithful servant*
Prov 31:10–13,19–20,30–31; Ps 127(128); I Thess 5:1–6; MATTHEW 25:14–30 (or 14–15,19–21)

2 Accept O Father
11 All that I am
135 In bread we bring you
181 Lord of all hopefulness
268 Reap me the earth (PG)
397 Almighty Father
483 God our maker, mighty Father (cf 1R)
545 Lord, in everything I do (PG)
547 Lord of creation (PG)

608 Take my life
637 Upon this table, Lord (PG)
650 What would you ask of me?
726 As a tree planted
739 Father, we come to you (E/G)
781 Centre of my life
782 O most high and glorious God
798 The kingdom of God (CT/R)

Your choice....

Sunday 34 *Come, you blessed of my Father*

Ezekiel 34:11–12,15–17; Ps 22(23); I Cor 15:20–26,28; MATTHEW 25:31–46

NB. Settings of Ps 22(23) may be found under Sunday 28

42	Christ is King of earth and heaven (E/G)	605	Sing to the world (CT/R)
43	Christ is our King (CT/R)	613	The King shall come (E/G)
56	Crown him with many crowns (CT/R)	626	This is the feast of victory
107	Hail, Redeemer, King divine	715	Christus vincit (CT/R)
168	Let all the world	731	Come, rejoice (E/G)
253	O worship the King (E/G)	734	Come, we that love the Lord
265	Praise we now the Lord our God (CT/R)	763	Jesus, lead the way
270	Rejoice! the Lord is king (E/G)	820	When the King shall come again
332	To Christ the Lord of worlds (E/G)	824	You are the king of glory
352	Whatsoever you do (Gosp)	826	You have put on Christ (2R)

Your choice....

Year B: Advent to Pentecost

Advent-Christmastide, Year B

Year B is the Year of Mark. This Gospel, however, does not have an 'infancy narrative' like Matthew's or Luke's, but begins with Jesus as a grown man. Its marvellously to-the-point opening words (1:1–8) are read on the 2nd Sunday of Advent, and taken up again (1:7–11) on the feast of the Baptism of the Lord.

To relate the incidents of Christ's birth, therefore, the liturgy has to borrow from one of the other Gospels, in this case Luke. The Gospel for the 4th Sunday of Advent is that of the Annunciation (Lk 1:26–38), while on the feast of the Holy Family, the Presentation in the Temple (Lk 2:22–40) provides the subject of the Gospel.

The themes of the Sundays of Advent follow the pattern set in Year A (see p.29).
1st Sunday: the second coming of Christ
2nd and 3rd Sundays: John the Baptist preaches
4th Sunday: the approaching birth of our Lord.

In Year B the 1st Sunday is rather sombre in tone, in contrast with years A or C. But the 2nd Sunday at once redresses the balance by beginning 'Console my people, console them.'

NOTES

1. Asterisked hymns may be used on more than one Sunday in a particular season.
2. Some hymns are based on one or other of the Readings of the day and these are noted as follows: 1R = First Reading; 2R = Second Reading; Gosp = Gospel;
3. Suggestions for the use of the hymns at Mass are noted thus (note that these are *suggestions* only): E/G = Entrance/Gathering; PG = Preparation of Gifts; Comm = Communion; R = Recessional, CT/R = Communion Thanksgiving or Recessional.
4. If you need EXTRA HYMNS: see p.27
5. Learning NEW HYMNS: see p.24
6. Space is provided after each Sunday for your own choice of hymns. Good ideas should be written down straight away so they are not forgotten.

Advent-Christmastide Hymns, Year B

Advent 1 *Give us life that we may call upon your name*
Isaiah 63:16–17; 64:1,3–8; Ps 79(80); I Cor 1:3–9; MARK 13:33–37

61	Dear maker of the starry skies (E/G)	587	Rain down justice (E/G)
112	Hark! a herald voice	591	Return to the Lord (E/G)
166	Let all mortal flesh keep silence(PG)	613	The King shall come (E/G)
173	Little flower in the ground	640	Wake up! the dawn is near (CT/R)
191	Many times I have turned (Pen.Rite)	*711	Ostende nobis, Domine (E/G)
227	O Lord my God, when I in awesome wonder	732	Come, Saviour, come (E/G)
233	O Jesus Christ, remember (CT/R)	733	Come to set us free (E/G)
267	Promised Lord and Christ	739	Father, we come to you (E/G)
480	God is working his purpose out (E/G)	771	My soul cannot be still
537	Like a sea without a shore	*805	Wait for the Lord (E/G)
540	Look around you (Pen.Rite)	*AK45	Gosp.Acc

Your choice....

Advent 2 *Prepare a way for the Lord!*
Isaiah 40:1–5,9–11; Ps 84(84); 2 Peter 3:8–14; MARK 1:1–8

16	A voice cries in the wilderness = AK71	639	Wake, awake! for night is dying
239	On Jordan's band the Baptist's cry	676	Psalm 84(85) (Resp Ps)
385	Across the years there echoes	*733	Come to set us free
436	Come, Lord Jesus	*742	For you, O Lord
439	Come, thou long-expected Jesus	789	Prepare ye the way of the Lord (E/G)
448	Fashion me a people	820	When the King shall come again (CT/R)
498	Hills of the north, rejoice	823	You shall go out with joy (CT/R)
563	Now watch for God's coming	AK25	(cf R.Ps), *45, 71, 77
566	O comfort my people (1R)		

Your choice....

Advent 3 *Good news to the poor*
Isaiah 61:1–2,10–11; Luke 1:46–50,53–4; I Thess 5:16–24; JOHN 1:6–8,19–28
* Settings of the Magnificat: more under Advent 4

110	Hail to the Lord's anointed (E/G)	437	Come, O divine Messiah
242	Open your ears, O Christian people (E/G)	*479	God has gladdened my heart
269	Rejoice in the Lord always	531	Lest he be too far from us
310	The King of glory comes	639	Wake, awake! for night is dying
319	The Spirit of the Lord is now upon me	*694	The Magnificat (cf Resp Ps)
405	Awake, awake! (E/G)	798	The Kingdom of God
*414	Breathing the words of humble obedience	800	The voice of God goes out (E/G)
426	Christ is coming	AK24	
428	Christ is the world's light		

Your choice....

Advent 4 *Listen! you are to conceive and bear a son*

2 Sam 7:1–5,8–12,14,16; Ps 88(89); Romans 16:25–27; LUKE 1:26–38

126 Holy Virgin, by God's decree (R)
*142 I sing the Lord God's praises (E)
216 O come, O come Emmanuel
301 The coming of our God
381 A noble flower of Juda
382 A sign is seen in heaven
*414 Breathing the words of humble obedience
437 Come, O divine Messiah!
465 Freely I give to you

490–2 Hail Mary
555 Mother of Jesus
572 Of one that is so fair and bright
*609 Tell out, my soul (E/G)
*694 The Magnificat
725 Awake, awake
*749 Great is the Lord
810 We have a King who comes
AK14, 74

Your choice....

Christmas and the feasts of Christmastide which do not change are to be found under Year A, p.31. The following days have alternative readings for Year B but you should check which ones are actually going to be used.

Holy Family *The Lord remembers his covenant for ever*

Optional Readings for Year B: Genesis 15:1–6; 21:1–3; Ps 104(105); Heb 11:8,11–12,17–19; LUKE 2:22–40 (or 22,39–40) See Year A; also

184 Love divine
235 O little town
382 A sign is seen in heaven
421 Child in the manger
553 May the peace of the Lord
568 O lady, full of God's own grace
573 Oh the word of my Lord

605 Sing to the world of Christ
614 The light of Christ
636 Unite us, Lord, in peace
649 What child is this
695 The Nunc Dimittis (cf Gosp)
755 I rejoiced when I heard them say
802 Those who were in the dark

Your choice....

The Baptism of the Lord *Come to the water*

Isaiah 55:1–11; Isaiah 12:2–6; I John 5:1–9; MARK 1:7–11

For the Blessing of Water:
    Water of Life (Eucharist section)
430 Christ the Lord has come

Hymns
 28 At the name of Jesus
208 Now come to me
286 Songs of thankfulness (not v.5)
400 As earth that is dry
439 Come, thou long-expected Jesus
518 In the beginning all was empty
524 Jesus the Lord has lived among us

531 Lest be be too far from us
614 The light of Christ (E/G)
619 The Spirit of God rests upon me
651 When Jesus comes to be baptised
724 All the ends of the earth (E/G)
768 Lord, the light of your love (CT/R)
806 Be here among us (CT/R)
814 We shall draw water
819 When John baptised
AK24

Your choice....

Lent and Eastertide, Year B

Before starting to plan for Lent, make sure what readings are being used for Sundays 3 to 5; on these days, the year A readings are used at Masses when the Scrutinies are held.

The great Year A Gospels from John are the classic Lent texts. But in all three years the Lent readings are taken from passages of great significance. In Lent, Year B, the First Readings of Sundays 1–3 are:

   Sun 1: Noah and the flood (Gen 9:8–15; parallel in Reading 2, I Pet 3:18–22)
   Sun 2: Abraham and Isaac (Gen 22; which is also the (neglected) second reading of the Easter Vigil)
   Sun 3: The Ten Commandments (Exodus 20:1–17).

The Gospel readings for Lent Sundays 3–5 are, as usual, from John:

   3: Moneylenders in the temple; 'I will raise it up in three days' (2:13–15)
   4: Jesus talks to Nicodemus: 'God so loved the world' (3:14–21)
   5: Jesus says 'Unless a grain of wheat shall fall' (12:20–33)

Note that the four Gospels, Sundays 2 to 5, all contain allusions to Jesus' passion and death.

In Eastertide, B, all the second readings are from the same book, I John. Read them and you will find them full of familiar phrases about the love of God. This letter goes well with John's Gospel which as usual is read at every Sunday in Easter, except for Sunday 3 which is from Luke and concerns the sequel to the Emmaus story. The first readings are from the Acts of the Apostles as usual.

Asterisked hymns may be used on more than one Sunday of the season.

Ash Wednesday *See Year A, p.34*

Lent 1 *Repent, and believe the Good News*
Genesis 9:8–15; Ps 24(25); I Peter 3:18–22; MARK 1:12–15

Blessing of Water:
   Water of Life (Eucharist section)
757 In the abundance of your compassion

Hymns and songs
 25 Attend and keep this happy fast (E/G)
 69 Father and life-giver
 80 Forty days and forty nights
104 Guide me, O thou great Redeemer (CT/R)
150 Jesu, lover of my soul
160 Keep we the fast (E/G)
165 Lead us, heavenly Father
*180 Lord Jesus, think on me
*183 Lord, who throughout these forty days
191 Many times I have turned

Your choice....

228 Oh holy Lord, by all adored (PG)
230 Oh the Lord looked down (for children?)
577 Our Father, we have wandered (E/G)
598 Show me your ways
632 To be the body of the Lord
660 You, Israel, return now
663 You shall cross the barren desert
669 Ps 24(25) (cf Resp Ps)
760 In your love remember me (cf Resp Ps) = AK15
771 My soul cannot be still = AK5
780 O Lord, be not mindful (Pen. Rite)
*788 Praise to you, O Christ (Gosp Acc)
798 The Kingdom of God (CT/R)
AK1, 3, 5, 15, 20, *46 (Gosp Acc)

Lent 2 *Tell no one what you have seen, until after the Son of Man has risen from the dead*
Gen 22:1–2,9–13.15–18; Ps 115(116); Rom 8:31–34; MARK 9:2–10

28 At the name of Jesus	530 Leave your country and your people
35 Be thou my vision	570 O raise your eyes on high
36 Blest are the pure in heart	641 We are bound for the promised land
46 Come, adore this wondrous presence	670 Psalm 26(27) (with Response 3)
65 Draw nigh and take the body	683 Psalm 114/5 (Resp Ps)
73 Fight the good fight	737 Eye has not seen
95 Godhead here in hiding	739 Father we come to you (E/G)
134 Immortal, invisible	748 God, your glory we have seen (CT/R)
167 Let all that is within me cry Holy	764 Jesus, Lord of life and love
428 Christ is the world's light	768 Lord, the light of your love
463 For to those who love God (2R)	773 Nothing can ever take away (2R)
515 If God is for us (2R)	815 We walk by faith
516 If God is our defender (2R)	★AK46

Your choice....

Lent 3 *In three days I will raise up this sanctuary*
When Year A readings are used (for the Scrutiny rite) see p.35
Ex 20:1–17 (or 1–3,7–8,12–17); Ps 18(19); I Cor 1:22–25; JOHN 2:13–25

17 Almighty Father (PG)	544 Lord, graciously hear us
167 Let all that is within me	549 Lord, thy word abideth
178 Lord, for tomorrow	658 Would you like to be happy (for children)
179 Lord, Jesus Christ	666 Psalm 18(19) (Resp Ps)
183 Lord, who throughout these forty days	730 Christ triumphant
201 My God, accept my heart	801 The word of God (cf Resp Ps) = AK11
226 Oh Lord, all the world belongs to you	AK11, ★46, 51
471 Give us the will to listen	

Your choice....

Lent 4 *God so loved the world that he sent his only Son*
When Year A readings are used (for the Scrutiny rite) see p.36
2 Chron 36:14–16,19–23; Ps 136(137); Eph 2:4–10; JOHN 3:14–21

90 Glory to thee, Lord God (R)	428 Christ is the world's light
94 God everlasting, wonderful and holy	577 Our Father, we have wandered (E/G)
97 God is love, his the care	614 The light of Christ
130 I believe in God the Father	660 You, Israel, return now
191 Many times I have turned	727 Before the heaven and earth
227 O Lord my God, when I in awesome wonder	730 Christ triumphant (CT/R)
234 O King of might and splendour (PG)	803 To God be the glory (CT/R)
338 Vaster far than any ocean	★AK46
405 Awake, awake! fling off the night (E/G)	

Your choice....

Lent 5 *If anyone serves me, they must follow me*
When Year A readings are used (for the Scrutiny rite) see p.36
Jeremiah 31:31–34; Ps 50(51); Hebrews 5:7–9; JOHN 12:20–23

60 Dear Lord and Father of mankind	454 Father of Heaven, whose love profound
73 Fight the good fight	(E/G)
88 Glory be to Jesus	489 Greater love has no man
184 Love divine	542 Lord, graciously hear us
217 O Father, now the hour has come (see	591 Return to the Lord
Tunefinder)	623 This is my body (CT/R)
224 O God, we give ourselves today	673 Psalm 50(51) (Resp Ps)
275 See us, Lord, about thine altar	748 God, your glory we have seen
288 Soul of my Saviour	774 Lord, you can open (2nd Alt. Resp) (Comm)
332 To Christ the Lord of worlds	812 Unless a grain of wheat (Comm/CT)
333 To Christ the Prince of Peace	AK20 (Resp Ps), *46, 66

Your choice....

Holy Week and Easter Day

See Year A, p.36

General Eastertide: *See p. 39*

Easter 2 *Thomas acknowledges the risen Jesus.*
Acts 4:32–35; Ps 117(118); I John 5:1–6; JOHN 20:19–31

56 Crown him with many crowns (v3: Gosp)	686 Psalm 117(118) (Resp Ps)
95 Godhead here in hiding (v.4: Gosp)	735 Confitemini Domino (E/G)
302 The day of resurrection	756 If God should lead us (CT)
364 Ye sons and daughters (vv.8–9)	762 Jesus is Lord (CT/R)
433 Come, God's people (E/G)	815 We walk by faith
493 He is Lord	AK33 (Resp Ps), 47 (Gosp Acc)

Your choice....

Easter 3 *It is written that Christ would suffer, and rise on the third day*
Acts 3:13–15,17–19; Ps 4: I John 2:1–5; Luke 24:35–48

42 Christ is King of earth and heaven	543 Lord, enthroned in heavenly splendour
187 Loving shepherd of thy sheep	571 O what a gift (v.8) (CT/R)
344 We celebrate this festive day (E/G)	787 Praise now your God (CT/R)
403 As one body (Comm)	803 To God be the glory (CT/R)

Your choice....

Easter 4 *The Good Shepherd lays down his life for his sheep*
Acts 4:8–12; Ps 117(118); I John 3:1–2; JOHN 10:11–18

10 All people that on earth do dwell	597 Shepherd of souls
27 At the Lamb's high feast	615 The Lord is my shepherd
107 Hail, Redeemer	667 Psalm 22 (23) (Comm/CT)
187 Loving shepherd	744 Forth in the peace (v5 cf Gosp)
249 O Thou who at thy Eucharist	793 Sing, all creation (E/G)
266 Praise we our God with joy	795 Sing it in the valley = AK84
311 The King of love	AK33 (cf Resp Ps), 66, 81, 84
312 The Lord's my shepherd	

Your choice....

Easter 5 *I am the vine, you are the branches*
Acts 9:26–31; Ps 21(22); I John 3:18–24; JOHN 15:1–8

244 O praise ye the Lord	579 Our Saviour Jesus Christ (v.4 cf Gosp)
307 The green life rises	811 We have been told
327 This is my will	812 Unless a grain of wheat (Comm/CT)
344 We celebrate this festive day (E/G)	825 You are the vine = AK67
424 Christ is alive (see v.4)	AK66, 67
502 I am the vine	

Your choice....

Easter 6 *Greater love has no man than to lay down his life*
Acts 10:25–26,34–35,44–48; Ps 97(98); I John 4:7–10; JOHN 15:9–17

S3 Now the green blade	581 Peace is my parting gift (vv5,7: end of Gosp)
76 Follow Christ (v3 cf Gosp)	623 This is my body, broken for you
96 God is love (2R)	628 This is what Yahweh asks
97 God is love (2R)	724 All the ends of the earth (cf Resp Ps) (E/G)
185 Love is his word	772 New songs of celebration (cf Resp Ps)
327 This is my will	792 Sing a new song (cf Resp Ps) (E/G)
380 A new commandment	811 We have been told
489 Greater love has no man	AK29 (cf Resp Ps), 66
510 I will be with you (cf end of Gosp)	

Your choice....

Ascension *Jesus at the right hand of God*
Acts 1:1–11; Ps 46(47); Eph 4:1–13 (or 1–7,11–13); MARK 16:15–20
The 2nd Reading from Year A may be read instead

7 Alleluia, sing to Jesus	429 Christ is the world's redeemer (see Tunefinder)
28 At the name of Jesus	
108 Hail the day that sees him rise	493 He is Lord
207 New praises be given	510 I will be with you
270 Rejoice! the Lord is King!	525 Jesus, you are Lord
308 The head that once was crowned	703 Go out to the whole world (round)

708 Let us go forth (round)
714 Stand and stare not (round)
727 Before the heaven and earth
730 Christ triumphant

748 God, your glory we have seen
762 Jesus is Lord
AK31 (cf Psalm)

Your choice....

Easter 7 *Consecrate them in the truth*
Acts 1:15–17,20–26; Ps 102(103); I John 4:11–16; JOHN 17:11–19

7 Alleluia, sing to Jesus
139 Into one we all are gathered
249 O thou, who at thy eucharist
429 Christ is the world's redeemer
383 Abba, abba, Father (cf Gosp)
470 Give praise to the Lord

525 Jesus, you are Lord
543 Lord, enthroned in heavenly splendour
681 Psalm 102(103) (Resp Ps)
728 Bless the Lord (cf Resp Ps) (E/G)
762 Jesus is Lord (CT/R)
809 We have a gospel to proclaim (CT/R)

Your choice....

Pentecost *Send forth your Spirit, O Lord*
Acts 2:1–11; Ps 103(104); Galatians 5:16–25; JOHN 15:26–27; 16:12–15
The 2nd Reading and Gospel from Year A may be read instead

49 Come down, O love divine
50 Come, holy Ghost
124 Holy Spirit, Lord of light (Sequence)
125 Holy Spirit of fire
225 Oh living water
289 Spirit of the living God
384 Abba, Father, send your Spirit
451 Father in heaven
453 Father, Lord of all creation (see v.3)
595/6 Send forth your Spirit

617 The Spirit is moving
625 This is the day
638 Veni, sancte Spiritus (E/G)
657 Wind and fire
682 Psalm 103(104) Resp. Psalm
700 Breath of life (round)
720 Veni creator Spiritus (E/G)
744 Forth in the peace of Christ (CT/R)
797 The gift of the Holy Spirit (CT/R)
AK32 (cf Psalm), 44 (Gosp Acc)

Your choice....

Trinity *In the name of the Father, and of the Son, and of the Holy Spirit*
Deut 4:32–34,39–40; Ps 32(33); Rom 8:14–17; MATTHEW 28:16–20

70 Father most holy
75 Firmly I believe and truly
121 Holy God, we praise thy name (E/G)
122/3 Holy, holy, holy (E/G)
130 I believe in God the Father
165 Lead us, heavenly Father
194 Merrily on
198 Most ancient of all mysteries

284 Sing praises to the living God
451 Father in heaven
452 Father, in my life
453 Father, Lord of all creation
455 Father, we praise you, now the night is over (E/G)
459 Firm is our faith
702 Glory be to God the Father (round)

64

703 Go out to the whole world (round) (CT/R)
708 Let us go forth (round)
744 Forth in the peace of Christ (CT/R)
Your choice....

797 The gift of the Holy Spirit (CT/R)
823 You shall go out with joy (CT/R)
AK85

The Body and Blood of Christ (Corpus Christi)
As they were eating he took some bread
Exodus 24:3–8; Ps 115(116); Hebrews 9:11–15; MARK 14:12–16,22–26

65   Draw nigh and take
74   Fill my house
218 O Father, take in sign of love
219 Of the glorious body telling
224 O Lord, we give ourselves today
249 O thou who at thy Eucharist (CT/R)
264 Praise to the Lord, the Almighty (PG)
324 They say I am wise
399 An upper room
403 As one body (Comm)
408 Before Christ died
412 Bread of the world (for choir use?)
438 Come, O Lord, to my heart
469 Gifts of bread and wine (PG)
501 I am the bread of life
521 Jesus said 'I am the bread'
Your choice....

523 Jesus the Lord said 'I am the bread'
543 Lord enthroned in heavenly splendour (CT/ R)
567 O food of travellers
597 Shepherd of souls (CT/R)
623 This is my body
648 Welcome, all ye noble saints
653 When the time came (E/G)
683 Ps 114/5 (cf Resp Ps)
764 Jesus, Lord of life and love
765 Jesus, you're the one I love = AK69
774 Now in this banquet (CommCT)
787 Praise now your God (CT/R)
802 Those who were in the dark
Eucharist Section: Lamb of God 2–4
AK51, 66, 68, 69

Sacred Heart *God is love*
Hosea 11:1,3–4,8–9; Isaiah 12:2–6; Eph 3:8–12,14–19; JOHN 19:31–37

15   All ye who seek a comfort sure
27   At the Lamb's high feast
96   God is love
97   God is love, his the care
150 Jesu, lover of my soul
161 King of glory, King of peace
248 O Sacred Heart
260 Praise, my soul (cf Resp Ps)
275 See us, Lord, about thine altar
288 Soul of my Saviour
293 Sweet heart of Jesus
333 To Christ, the Prince of peace
Your choice....

334 To Jesus' heart all-burning
355 When I survey
404 As the bridegroom
471 Give us the will to listen
499 His light now shines
592 Rock of ages
696 Adoramus te, Domine
728 Bless the Lord, my soul (cf Resp Ps)
765 Jesus, you're the one I love = AK 69
777 O Christe Domine Jesu
814 We shall draw water (Resp Ps)
AK70, 77, 79

Ordinary Time, Year B

The Gospel of Mark is written in a direct and vivid style, such as an eye-witness would use. There is an old tradition that Mark wrote down the memories and preaching of St Peter, and this is thought to be quite probable.

For this and other reasons, Mark's is generally thought to be the earliest Gospel, composed some time between 64 and 70 AD.

It is also the shortest Gospel and is often dismissed as of less interest than Matthew or Luke. In fact Mark has a definite viewpoint. The first half of the Gospel (up to chapter 8) shows Jesus working many signs and teaching 'with authority' (Sunday 4), but at the same time meeting with incomprehension. Jesus also frequently tells people who recognise him not to say anything about him (Sunday 6,13). This has become known as the 'Messianic Secret'.

There is a turning point in chapter 8, when Peter confesses Jesus to be the Christ (Sunday 24). After this the emphasis of the Gospel changes, and it becomes a catechism on true discipleship, in which Jesus progressively teaches the apostles about the nature of his task and theirs. He prophesies his death and resurrection (Sunday 25) – characteristically, the disciples do not understand.

In the middle of year B (Sundays 17–21) there is an interlude in which chapter 6 of the Gospel of John is read, spread over five Sundays. This is an extended teaching on the Eucharist, and such a 'block' is unique in the three-year cycle. But for the rest, hear Mark proclaim 'the good news about Jesus Christ, the Son of God' (1:1)

NOTES

1. Asterisked hymns may be used on more than one Sunday in a particular season.
2. Some hymns are based on one or other of the Readings of the day and these are noted as follows: 1R = First Reading; 2R = Second Reading; Gosp = Gospel;
3. Suggestions for the use of the hymns at Mass are noted thus (note that these are *suggestions* only): E/G = Entrance/Gathering; PG = Preparation of Gifts; Comm = Communion; R = Recessional, CT/R = Communion Thanksgiving or Recessional.
4. If you need EXTRA HYMNS: see p.27
5. Learning NEW HYMNS: see p.24
6. Space is provided after each Sunday for your own choice of hymns. Good ideas should be written down straight away so they are not forgotten.

Sunday 2 *Speak, Lord, your servant is listening*

1 Sam 3:3–10,19; Ps 39(40); I Cor 6:13–15,17–20; JOHN 1:35–42

s1	God gives his people strength	545	Lord, in everything I do (PG)
11	All that I am (PG)	574	Oh the word of my Lord
78/744	Forth in the peace of Christ (CT/R)	608	Take my life
79	Forth in thy name (CT/R)	632	To be the body of the Lord
142	I sing the Lord God's praises (see Tunefinder)	635	Trust in the Lord
		747	God who spoke in the beginning (see Tunefinder)
201	My God, accept my heart (PG)		
224	O God we give ourselves today	766	Jubilate everybody (E/G)
296	Take my hands (PG)	781	Centre of my life
327	This is my will (see v.4)	758	In the Lord (E/G)
388	All for Jesus (comm)	816	What do you want of me
496	He's a most unusual man	AK18	(cf Resp Ps), 76
508	Here I am, Lord		**Your choice....**

66

Sunday 3 *He called them at once and they went after him*
Jonah 3:1–5,10; Ps 24(25); I Cor 7:29–31; MARK 1:14–20

51 Come, Lord Jesus, come
60 Dear Lord and Father of mankind
99 Go tell everyone (CT/R)
119 He who would valiant be
172 Light of our darkness
296 We are one in the Spirit (CT/R)
456 Fear not, for I have redeemed you
460 Follow me
463 For to those who love God
506 I met you at the cross

550 Lord, you have come to the lakeside
593 Seek ye first the kingdom
598 Show me your ways
744 Forth in the peace of Christ (CT/R)
760 In your love = AK15
748 God, your glory we have seen (CT/R)
775 O changeless Christ
785 One shall tell another
AK15

Your choice....

Sunday 4 *His teaching made a deep impression because he taught with authority*
Deut 18:15–20; Ps 94(95); I Cor 7:32–35; MARK 1:21–28

64 Do you know that the Lord walks on earth
141 I will sing a song
172 Light of our darkness
242 Open your ears O Christian people
379 A mighty stronghold
435 Come, let us sing (cf Resp Ps;) (E/G)
524 Jesus the Word has lived among us
531 Lest he be too far from us
605 Sing to the world (CT/R)

610 That which we have heard
614 The light of Christ (E/G)
629 Thou whose almighty Word (E/G)
679 Psalm 94 (95) (Resp Ps)
783 O that today (cf Resp Ps) = AK28
792 Sing a new song to the Lord (E/G)
824 You are the King of glory (CT/R)
AK28   (cf Resp Ps)

Your choice....

Sunday 5 *He went all through Galilee, preaching and casting out devils*
Job 7:1–4,6–7; Ps 146; I Cor 9:16–19,22–23

6 Alleluia, I will praise the Father
32 Be still, and know I am with you
43 Christ is our King
76 Follow Christ and love the world
145 I watch the sunrise
190 Man of Galilee
208 Now come to me all you who seek
231 Oh the love of my Lord
310 The king of glory comes
428 Christ is the world's light

436 Come, Lord Jesus, come
470 Give praise to the Lord (E/G)
528 Lay your hands gently upon us
579 Our Saviour Jesus Christ proclaimed
664 The eyes of the blind
752 Here in this place (CT/R)
774 Now in this banquet (Comm/CT)
799 The master came (also for Sunday 6)
808 We give God thanks

Your choice....

Sunday 6 *Happy the man whose offence is forgiven. If you want, you can cure me*

Lev 13:1–2,44–46; Ps 31(32); I Cor 10:31–11:1; MARK 1:40–45

Blessing of water:
757 In the abundance; AK1

6 Alleluia! I will praise the Father
19 Amazing grace
150 Jesu, lover of my soul
158 Jesus, thou art coming
191 Many times I have turned
260 Praise, my soul, the king of heaven
338 Vaster far than any ocean

434 Come, Holy Lord, our faith renew
447 Faith in God can move the mountains
528 Lay your hands gently upon us
739 Father we come to you
776 O Christ the healer
770 My people, I hear you calling (E/G)
780 O Lord, be not mindful (Pen Rite)
794 Sing of the Lord's goodness
813 We're forgiven (also for Sunday 7)
AK1,3

Your choice....

Sunday 7 *Who can forgive sins but God?*

Isaiah 43:18–19,21–22,24–25; Ps 40(41); 2 Cor 1:18–22; MARK 2:1–2

Some hymns from last week are useful; also
81 From the deep I lift my voice
223 O God thy people gather (E/G)
447 Faith in God
454 Father of heaven, whose love profound (E/G)
466 From the depths of sin and sadness (E/G)
473 Glory and praise to our God (CT/R)

477 God forgave my sin (CT/R)
544 Lord, graciously hear us
764 Jesus, Lord of life and love
765 Bread, blessed and broken = AK69
797 The gift of the Holy Spirit (CT/R)
813 We're forgiven
AK69

Your choice....

Sunday 8 *Rejoice while the bridegroom is with you*

Hosea 2:16–17,21–2; Ps 102(103); 2 Cor 3:1–6; MARK 2:18–22

54 Come to the Lord
74 Fill my house
90 Glory to thee, Lord God (CT/R)
97 God is love, his the care (E/G)
161 King of glory, king of peace
202 My God, and is thy table spread
266 Praise we our God with joy (CT/R)
269 Rejoice in the Lord always
402 As long as men on earth
404 As the bridegroom (CT/R)
469 Gifts of bread and wine (PG)
470 Give praise to the Lord (E/G)
499 His light now shines
513 I will tell of your love
523 Jesus the Lord said

524 Jesus the Word has lived among us
539 Look around, look around you
578 Our help is the name of the Lord (cf Resp Ps) (E/G)
648 Welcome all ye noble saints
681 Ps 102 (103) (Resp Ps)
728 Bless the Lord, my soul (cf Resp Ps) (E/G)
750 Who calls my life (cf Resp Ps)
763 Jesus, lead the way
764 Jesus, Lord of life and love
765 Jesus, you're the one I love
787 Praise now your God (CT/R)
774 Now in this banquet (Comm)
795 Sing it in the valleys = AK84
AK31 (cf Resp Ps), 84

Your choice....

Sunday 9 *The Son of Man is Lord even of the sabbath*
Deut 5:12–15; Ps 80(81); 2 Cor 4:6–11; MARK 2:23–3:6 (or 2:23–28)

10 All people that on earth (E)	585 Praise the Lord! ye heavens adore him
14 All this world belongs to Jesus	731 Come, rejoice before your maker (E/G)
23 Ask and you whall receive	747 God who spoke in the beginning
131 I danced in the morning (v3 cf Gosp)	762 Jesus is Lord
156 Jesus is God!	761 It is good to give thanks (E/G)
344 We celebrate this festive day (E/G)	799 The master came (CT/R)
345 We gather together (E/G)	804 To Jesus Christ our sovereign King (CT/R)
386 Again the Lord's own day is here (E/G)	822 You are the Lord (CT/R)
467 Gather, Christians (E/G)	AK19

Your choice....

Sunday 10 *All men's sins will be forgiven... anyone who does the will of God is my brother and sister and mother*
Genesis 3:9–15; Ps 129(130); 2 Cor 4:13–5:1; MARK 3:20–35

7 Alleluia! sing to Jesus	477 God forgave my sin (CT/R)
81 From the deep (cf Resp Ps)	496 He's a most unusual man
119 He who would valiant be	577 Our Father, we have wandered (E/G)
165 Lead us, heavenly Father, lead us	593 Seek ye first
191 Many times I have turned (E/G)	689 Psalm 129 (130) (Resp Ps)
223 O God thy people gather (E/G)	746 God is my great desire
228 O holy Lord, by all adored (PG)	750 Who calls my life again
379 A mighty stronghold	770 My people, I hear you calling (E/G)
466 From the depths of sin and sadness (cf Resp Ps)	773 Nothing can ever take away from us
	AK 36 (cf Resp Ps)

Your choice....

Sunday 11 *What can we say the Kingdom of Heaven is like?*
Ezekiel 17:22–24; Ps 91(92); 2 Cor 5:6–10; MARK 4:26–34

42 Christ is King of earth and heaven (E/G)	612 The church is wherever
111 Happy the man	670 One thing I ask (cf Comm. Antiphon)
138 In the earth the small seed	696 The Beatitudes
307 The green life rises	726 As a tree planted
320 The Kingdom (= AK 73)	729 Christ's Church shall glory
457 Fear not, rejoice and be glad	748 God, your glory (v.1 cf Gosp) (CT/R)
478 God gives us harvest (PG)	761 It is good to give thanks (cf Resp Ps)
520 It's good to give thanks (cf Resp Ps)	AK73

Your choice....

69

Sunday 12 *Who can this be? Even the wind and the sea obey him*
Job 38:1,8–11; Ps 106(107); 2 Cor 5:14–17; MARK 4:35–41

33	Be still and know	411	Blest be the Lord
67	Eternal Father, strong to save	447	Faith in God
117	He's got the whole world	456	Fear not, for I have redeemed you
156	Jesus is God!	585	Praise the Lord! ye heavens, adore him
165	Lead us, heavenly Father	615	The Lord is my shepherd
253	O worship the King (E/G)	663	You shall cross the barren desert
294	Sweet sacrament divine (Comm) (v.3 cf Gosp)	759	In the Lord I'll be ever thankful (E/G)
		761	It is good to give thanks (E/G)
340	Walk with me, O my Lord	762	Jesus is Lord! (CT/R)
407	Be still, my soul	775	O changeless Christ

Your choice....

Sunday 13 *O Lord, you have raised my soul from the dead*
Wisdom 1:13–5; 2:23–4; Ps 29(30); 2 Cor 8:7,9,13–15; MARK 5:21–43 (or 21–4,35–43)

9	All hail the power of Jesus' name	386	Again the Lord's own day
23	Ask and you shall receive	517	In God alone is there rest for my soul
43	Christ is our king	537	Like a sea without a shore
90	Glory to thee, Lord God	579	Our Saviour Jesus Christ proclaimed
134	Immortal, invisible	585	Praise the Lord! ye heavens, adore him
208	Now come to me, all you who seek (see Tunefinder)	604	Sing to the mountains (CT/R)
		728	Bless the Lord, my soul (E/G, Comm)
278	Sing my soul of his mercy	759	In the Lord (Comm)
284	Sing praises to the living God	781	Centre of my life
350	We will walk through the valley	813	We're forgiven
384	Abba Father, send your spirit (CT/R)		

Your choice....

Sunday 14 *All too full is our soul with the proud man's disdain*
Ezekiel 2:2–5; Ps 122(123); 2 Corinthians 12:7–10; MARK 6:1–6

35	Be thou my vision	508	Here I am, Lord
58	Day by day in the market place	531	Lest he be too far from us
64	Do you know that the Lord walks	635	Trust in the Lord
73	Fight the good fight	729	Christ's church shall glory
78/744	Forth in the peace of Christ (CT/R)	739	Father, we come to you (E/G)
111	Happy the man	744	see 78
119	He who would valiant be	753	How shall they hear the Word
324	They say I am wise	763	Jesus lead the way
411	Blest be the Lord	783	O that today = AK28
444	Do not be afraid		AK28
449	Father, hear the prayer we offer (PG)		

Your choice....

Sunday 15 *Go, prophesy to my people*
Amos 7:12–15; Ps 84(85); Eph 1:3–14 (or 3–10; MARK 6:7–13

Some from last week may be suitable; also:
s7   Lord, make me an instrument of thy peace
45   Colours of day
51   Come, Lord Jesus, come
76   Follow Christ and love the world
78/744 Forth in the peace of Christ
79   Forth in thy name (CT/R)
361   With a song in our hearts (CT/R)
508   Here I am, Lord
510   I will be with you (CT/R)
530   Leave your country

550   Lord, you have come to the lakeside
574   Oh the word of my Lord
629   Thou whose almighty Word (E/G)
656   Who wants to live as God
663   Be not afraid (CT/R)
676   Psalm 84(85) (cf Resp Ps)
703   Go out to the whole world (CT/R)
706/7 Jubilate Deo (E/G)
708   Let us go forth
809   We have a Gospel (CT/R)
AK25 (cf R Ps)

Your choice....

Sunday 16   *I will gather my flock*
Jeremiah 23:1–6; Ps 22(23); Eph 2:13–18; MARK 6:30–34

10   All people that on earth do dwell
181   Lord of all hopefulness
187   Loving shepherd of thy sheep
266   Praise we our God with joy (CT/R)
311   The King of love
312   The Lord's my shepherd
322   The wandering flock of Israel
450   Father I place into your hands (PG)
452   Father, in my life I see

511   I will never forget you
615   The Lord is my shepherd
667   Ps 22(23) Resp. Psalm
758   In the land there is a hunger
770   My people, I hear you (E/G)
777   O Christe Domine Jesu (E/G, Comm)
793   Sing, all creation (E/G)
797   The gift of the Holy Spirit (CT/R)
AK13 (cf Resp Ps)

Your choice....

Sunday 17   *You give us our food in due time*
Kings 2:42–44; Ps 144(145); Eph 4:1–6; JOHN 6:1–15

The Eucharist section from John begins here and continues till Sunday 21. Some hymns are suitable for more than one Sunday and it is a chance to introduce and learn new ones, or a new Eucharistic chant, e.g. Lamb of God.

17   Almighty Father, God most high
54   Come to the Lord
65   Draw nigh, and take
74   Fill my house
94   God everlasting
97   God is love, his the care (E/G)
171   Let us with a gladsome mind
535   Let us talents and tongues employ
543   Lord, enthroned in heavenly splendour
       (CT/R)
567   O food of travellers
597   Shepherd of souls (CT/R)
609   Tell out, my soul (CT/R)
621   There is one Lord (2R)

648   Welcome, all ye noble saints
683   Psalm 114: How can I repay the Lord?
690   Psalm 135: O give thanks to the Lord (CT)
691   Psalm 144(145) Resp.Psalm
752   Gather us in (E/G)
765   Jesus, you're the one I love
774   Now in this banquet (Comm/CT)
775   O changeless Christ
794   Sing of the Lord's goodness
798   The kingdom of God
802   Those who were in the dark
Eucharistic Section: Lamb of God 2–4
AK38 (cf Resp Ps), 68, 69

Your choice....

71

Sunday 18 *Do not work for bread that cannot last. I am the bread of life.*
Exodus 16:2–4,12–15; Ps 77(78); Eph 4:17,20–24; JOHN 6:24–35

7	Alleluia, sing to Jesus	501	I am the bread of life
54	Come to the Lord	605	Sing to the world (CT/R)
177	Lord, accept the gifts (PG)	643	We form one church (E/G)
186	Loving Father, from thy bounty (PG)	683	Psalm 114: How can I repay the Lord?
202	My God, and is thy table spread	690	Psalm 135: O give thanks to the Lord (CT)
324	They say I am wise	765	Jesus, you're the one I love
344	We celebrate this festive day (E/G)	774	Now in this banquet
400	As earth that is dry	787	Praise now your God
402	As long as men on earth	818	What is this place (E/G)
403	As one body		Eucharistic Section: Lamb of God 2–4
438	Come, O Lord, to my heart today		AK68, 69

Your choice....

Sunday 19 *Anyone who eats this bread will live for ever*
I Kings 19:4–8; Ps 33(34); Eph 4:30–5:2; JOHN 6:41–51

65	Draw nigh, and take the body of the Lord	501	I am the bread of life
69	Father and life-giver	534	Let us praise our sovereign Saviour
128	I am the bread of life	683	Psalm 114: How can I repay the Lord?
166	Let all mortal flesh (PG)	690	Psalm 135: O give thanks to the Lord (CT)
185	Love is his word	754	I received the living God (CT)
275	See us, Lord, about thine altar (Comm/CT)	774	Now in this banquet
403	As one body	818	What is this place (E)
412	Bread of the world		Eucharistic Section: Lamb of God 2–4

Your choice....

Sunday 20 *Anyone who eats this bread, I will raise up on the last day*
Proverbs 9:1–6; Ps 33(34); Eph 5:15–20; JOHN 6:51–58

95	Godhead here in hiding	523	Jesus the Lord said 'I am the bread'
179	Lord Jesus Christ	623	This is my body, broken for you
220	O Godhead hid	653	When the time came to lay down his life
224	O God, we give ourselves today	683	Psalm 114: How can I repay the Lord?
287	Sons of God, hear his holy word	754	I received the living God (CT)
307	The green life rises	690	Psalm 135: O give thanks to the Lord (CT)
403	As one body we are wed (Comm)	764	Jesus, Lord of life and love
408	Before Christ died	812	Unless a grain of wheat
469	Gifts of bread and wine (PG)		Eucharistic Section: Lamb of God 2–4
501	I am the bread of life		AK66

Your choice....

Sunday 21 *Lord, to whom shall we go?*
Joshua 24:1–2,15–18; Ps 33(34); Eph 5:21–32; JOHN 6:60–69

46	Come, adore this wondrous presence	227	O Lord my God, when I in awesome wonder
75	Firmly I believe	234	O King of might and splendour (PG)
95	Godhead here in hiding	288	Soul of my saviour

403 As one body (Comm)
496 He's a most unusual man
521 Jesus said 'I am the bread'
605 Sing to the world of Christ (CT/R)
696 Adoramus te, Domine (Comm)

754 I received the living God (CT)
764 Jesus, Lord of life and love
812 Unless a grain of wheat
Eucharistic Section: Lamb of God 2–4
AK66

Your choice....

Sunday 22 *True intentions come from the heart*
Deut 4:1–2,6–8; Ps 14(15); James 1:17–18,21–22,27; MARK 7:1–8,14–15,21–23

6 Alleluia! I will praise the Father
36 Blest are the pure in heart
37 Breathe on me, breath of God
60 Dear Lord and Father of mankind
76 Follow Christ and love the world
84 Give me joy in my heart
111 Happy the man
201 My God accept my heart (PG)
296 Take my hands (PG)
320 The Kingdom = AK73
417 But I say unto you

542 Lord, confronted with your might
545 Lord, in everything I do (PG)
557 My God, you fathom my heart
593 Seek ye first
598 Show me your ways
699 The Beatitudes
726 As a tree planted
760 In your love remember me = AK15
781 Centre of my life
798 The kingdom of God (CT/R)
801 The word of God = AK11
AK11, 14, 15, 73

Your choice....

Sunday 23 *The deaf hear and the dumb speak*
Isaiah 35:4–7; Ps 145(146); James 2:1–5; MARK 7:31–37

6 Alleluia! I will praise the Father (cf Resp Ps)
43 Christ is our King (v.4 cf Gosp)
190 Man of Galilee
260 Praise, my soul, the King of heaven
310 The King of glory comes
345 We gather together (E/G)
528 Lay our hands
579 Our Saviour Jesus Christ proclaimed
664 The eyes of the blind(1R)

728 Bless the Lord, my soul (E/G)
752 Gather us in (E/G)
774 Now in this banquet (Comm/CT)
775 O changeless Christ
776 O Christ the healer
799 The master came (CT/R)
813 We're forgiven
824 You are the King of glory (CT/R)
AK39 (cf Resp Ps)

Your choice....

Sunday 24 *Who do you say I am? You are the Christ (see introduction to Ordinary Time, Year B,*
Isaiah 50:5–9; Ps 114(115); James 2:14–18; MARK 8:27–35   *p.66)*

28 At the name of Jesus
64 Do you know that the Lord walks on earth
88 Glory be to Jesus
119 He who would valiant be
156 Jesus is God!
166 Let all mortal flesh (PG)
206 My song is love unknown = AK80
227 O Lord my God, when I in awesome wonder
325 This day God gives me
388 All for Jesus
415 Bright star of morning
418 Christ suffered for you

427 Christ is made the sure foundation (E/G)
429 Christ is the world's redeemer (see Tunefinder)
506 I met you at the cross
522 Jesus, the holy Lamb of God
526 Keep in mind (CT)
531 Lest he be too far from us
598 Show me your ways
605 Sing to the world (CT/R)
656 Who wants to live as God
683 Psalm 114(115) (Resp Ps)
707 Jubilate Deo (E/G or R)
727 Before the heaven and earth

730 Christ triumphant
762 Jesus is Lord (CT/R)
Your choice....

809 We have a Gospel (R)
822 You are the Lord
AK51, 80

Sunday 25 *The Lord upholds my life*
Wisdom 2:12,17–20; Ps 53(54); James 3:16–4:3; MARK 9:30–37

15   All ye who seek a comfort sure
51   Come, Lord Jesus, come
154 Jesus, gentlest Saviour (v.2 cf Gosp)
187 Loving shepherd of thy sheep
222 O God our help in ages past
292 Suffer little children (cf Gosp)
352 Whatsoever you do
362 Yahweh, you are my strength
379 A mighty stronghold
515 If God is for us
592 Rock of ages
Your choice....

598 Show me your ways
607 Son of the Father
615 The Lord is my shepherd
644 We gather together to ask the Lord (E/G)
630 Though the mountains may fall
656 Who wants to live as God
759 In the Lord I'll be ever thankful (E/G)
763 Jesus, lead the way
773 Nothing can ever take away from us
791 Safe in the shadow
AK21, 66

Sunday 26 *Anyone who is not against us is for us*
Numbers 11:25–29; Ps 18(19); James 5:1–6; MARK 9:38–43,45,47–48

36   Blest are the pure in heart
226 O Lord, all the world belongs to you
296 Take my hands
327 This is my will
342 We are one in the Spirit
397 Almighty Father, who for us (v.1 cf Gosp)
661 You must cry out the Word
666 Psalm 18(19) (Resp Ps)
Your choice....

703 Go out to the whole world (R)
708 Let us go forth
739 Father, we come to you (E/G)
744 Forth in the peace of Christ (CT/R)
753 How shall they hear the Word
797 The gift of the Holy Spirit (CT/R)
801 The word of God (cf Resp Ps) = AK11
AK11

Sunday 27 *They become one body*
Genesis 2:18–24; Ps 127(128); Hebrews 2:9–11; MARK 10:2–16 (or 2–12)

136 In Christ there is no East or West
139 Into one we all are gathered
185 Love is his word
240 On this house your blessing, Lord
243 O perfect love
342 We are one in the Spirit (CT/R)
345 We gather together as brothers and sisters
409 Bind us together   (E/G)
413 Break not the circle
Your choice....

450 Father, I place into your hands (PG)
583 Peacetime
602 Sing to the Lord a song (1R)
647 We thank you Father for the gift
741 For the beauty of the earth
782 O most high and glorious God
785 One shall tell another
786 Peace I give to you
AK83

Sunday 28 *That we may gain wisdom of heart*
Wisdom 7:7–11; Ps 89(90); Hebrews 4:12–13; MARK 10:17–30 (or 17–27)

11   All that I am
35   Be thou my vision
36   Blest are the pure in heart

37   Breathe on me, breath of God
41   Christ be beside me
78/744 Forth in the peace of Christ (CT/R)

74

201 My God, accept my heart (PG)
242 Open your ears, O Christian people (E/G)
397 Almighty Father, who for us
460 Follow me
509 I was born before creation (1R)
530 Leave your country and your people
547 Lord of creation (PG)
Your choice....

550 Lord, you have come to the lakeside
612 The Church is wherever
632 To be the body of the Lord
634 Together we journey
706/7 Jubilate Deo (E/G or R)
731 Come, rejoice (E/G)
781 Centre of my life
AK26 (cf Resp Ps)

Sunday 29 *Can you drink the cup that I must drink?*
Isaiah 53:10–11; Ps 32(33); Hebrews 4:14–16; MARK 10:35–45 (or 42–45)

218 O Father, take in sign of love (PG)
224 O God, we give ourselves today (PG)
227 O Lord my God, when I in awesome wonder
234 O King of might and splendour (PG)
296 Take my hands (PG)
355 When I survey the wondrous cross
418 By his wounds
526 Keep in mind
530 Leave your country and your people
Your choice....

608 Take my life (PG)
656 Who wants to live as God
730 Christ triumphant
739 Father, we come to you (E/G)
748 God, your glory we have seen (CT/R)
794 Sing of the Lord's goodness
795 Sing it in the valleys
798 The kingdom of God
803 To God be the glory (CT/R)
AK70 (cf 1R)

Sunday 30 *I will gather them all: the blind and the lame*
Jeremiah 31:7–9; Ps 125(126); Hebrews 5:1–6; MARK 10:46–52

6 Alleluia, I will praise the Father
35 Be thou my vision
43 Christ is our King
45 Colours of day
120 Holy Father, God of might (R)
140 I saw the grass
145 I watch the sunrise
190 Man of Galilee
260 Praise, my soul, the King of heaven
406 Bartimaeus (cf Gosp)
528 Lay your hands
Your choice....

579 Our Saviour Jesus Christ proclaimed
614 The light of Christ
664 The eyes of the blind
668 Ps 125(126) (Resp Ps)
752 Gather us in (E/G)
756 If God should lead us (cf Resp Ps)
774 Now in this banquet (Comm/CT)
792 Sing a new song to the Lord (E/G)
802 Those who sere in the dark
824 You are the King of glory (CT/R)
AK35 (cf Resp Ps), 77

Sunday 31 *What is the greatest of the commandments?*
Deut 6:2–6; Ps 17(18); Hebrews 7:23–28; MARK 12:28–34

139 Into one we all are gathered
152 Jesu, the very thought of thee
161 King of glory, King of peace
210 Now Jesus said (children)
327 This is my will
358 Where is love and loving-kindness
362 Yahweh, you are my strength (cf Resp Ps)
402 As long as men on earth
404 As the bridegroom to his chosen
415 Bright star of morning
Your choice....

435 Come, let us sing out our joy (E/G)
441 Day by day
442 Dear love of my heart
447 Faith in God
652 When morning gilds the skies (E/G)
658 Would you like to be happy (children)
746 God is my great desire
793 Sing, all creation (E/G)
822 You are the Lord
AK10 (cf Psalm), 21, 83

Sunday 32 *The poor are more generous than the rich*

I Kings 17:10–16; Ps 145(146); Hebrews 9:24–28; MARK 12:38–44 (or 41–44)

6	I will praise the Father (cf Resp Ps)	314	The prophet in his hunger (1R)
11	All that I am (PG)	320	The Kingdom = AK73
17	Almighty Father, Lord most high (PG)	351	What can we offer you (PG)
51	Come, Lord Jesus	478	God gives us harvest (PG)
72	Feed us now	637	Upon this table, Lord (PG)
134	Immortal, invisible (E/G)	650	What do you ask of me (PG)
208	Now come to me, all you who seek (E/G)	699	The Beatitudes
224	O God, we give ourselves (PG)	774	Now in this banquet (Comm/CT)
226	Oh Lord, all the world	797	The gift of the Holy Spirit
260	Praise, my soul, the King of heaven	801	The word of God = AK11
266	Praise we our God with joy (CT/R)		AK11, 39 (cf Resp Ps), 73
296	Take my hands (PG)		

Your choice....

Sunday 33 *In those days... they will see the Son of Man coming with great power and glory*

Daniel 12:1–3; Ps 15(16); Hebrews 10:11–14,18; MARK 13:24–32

36	Blest are the pure in heart	411	Blest be the Lord
136	In Christ there is no east or west	498	Hills of the north
166	Let all mortal flesh (PG)	630	Though the mountains may fall
184	Love divine, all loves excelling	635	Trust in the Lord
227	O Lord my God	640	Wake up! the dawn is near
233	O Jesus Christ, remember	711	Ostende nobis (E/G)
284	Sing praises to the living God	763	Jesus, lead the way
286	Songs of thankfulness (see v.4)	768	Shine, Jesus, shine (CT/R)
300	The Church's one foundation	781	Centre of my life (cf Resp Ps)
389	All for Jesus	820	When the King shall come again

Your choice....

Sunday 34 *Mine is not a kingdom of this world*

Daniel 7:13–14; Ps 92(93); Apocalypse 1:5–8; JOHN 18:33–37

4	All creatures of our God and king	435	Come, let us sing out our joy (E/G)
42	Christ is King of earth and heaven	470	Give praise to the Lord (E/G)
43	Christ is our King	605	Sing to the world (CT/R)
56	Crown him with many crowns	678	Ps 92(93) (Resp Ps)
107	Hail Redeemer, King divine	715	Christus vincit (CT/R)
121	Holy God, we praise thy name (E/G)	730	Christ triumphant
253	O worship the King (E/G)	734	Come we that love the Lord
270	Rejoice! the Lord is King	748	God, your glory we have seen (CT/R)
324	They say I am wise	762	Jesus is Lord!
332	To Christ the Lord of worlds	804	To Jesus Christ, our Sovereign King (CT/R)
391	All you nations (E/G)		AK23

Your choice....

Year C: Advent to Pentecost

Advent-Christmastide, Year C

Year C is the Year of Luke (see also the note for Ordinary Time). The keynote from the start (Advent 1) is optimism: 'Stand erect, hold your heads high, because your liberation is near at hand.' Luke's portrayal of Jesus is the most attractive of the four gospels, and he gives many instances of the mercy and gentleness of Christ. But these are balanced by a sense of urgency, of much to be accomplished in a short time; one of Luke's characteristic phrases is 'Stay awake, praying at all times.' He likes historical details – see the beginning of the Gospel for Advent 3. On Advent 4 the story of the Visitation appears for the only time in the Sunday cycle. John the Baptist appears as usual on Advent 2 and 3; other verses of the same chapter are read on the Baptism of the Lord, showing once again the close connection of this feast to Advent. The first reading on this day is a famous passage from Isaiah, usually known as 'the Advent prophet'. (In fact Year C departs from the usual pattern in that the first readings in Advent are taken from prophets other than Isaiah.)

NOTES

1. Asterisked hymns may be used on more than one Sunday in a particular season.
2. Some hymns are based on one or other of the Readings of the day and these are noted as follows: 1R = First Reading; 2R = Second Reading; Gosp = Gospel;
3. Suggestions for the use of the hymns at Mass are noted thus (note that these are *suggestions* only): E/G = Entrance/Gathering; PG = Preparation of Gifts; Comm = Communion; R = Recessional, CT/R = Communion Thanksgiving or Recessional.
4. If you need EXTRA HYMNS: see p.27
5. Learning NEW HYMNS: see p.24
6. Space is provided after each Sunday for your own choice of hymns. Good ideas should be written down straight away so they are not forgotten.

Advent-Christmastide Hymns, Year C

Advent 1 *See, the days are coming*
Jeremiah 33:14–16; Ps 24(25); I Thess 3:12–4:2; LUKE 21:25–28,34–36

45	Colours of day	669	Ps 24(25) (Resp Ps)
61	Dear maker of the starry skies	*733	Come to set us free
112	Hark! a herald voice is calling	760	In your love remember me
233	O Jesus Christ, remember	770	My people, I hear you
301	The coming of our God	777	O Christe Domine Jesu (+ Ps 24)
384	Abba, Father (with seasonal verses)	801	The Word of God (cf Resp Ps) = AK11
457	Fear not, rejoice and be glad	*805	Wait for the Lord (E/G)
480	God is working his purpose out	AK11	(cf Resp Ps), 45 (Gosp. Acc)
498	Hills of the north, rejoice		

Your choice....

Advent 2 *Arise, Jerusalem, stand on the heights*
Baruch 5:1–9; Ps 125(126); Phil 1:4–6,8–11. LUKE 3:1–6

16   A voice cries = AK71 (E/G)
239 On Jordan's bank
242 Open your ears, O Christian people
385 Across the years there echoes still
563 Now watch for God's coming
566 O comfort my people (E/G)

688 Ps 125(126) (Resp Ps)
752 Here in this place (E/G)
756 If God should lead us (cf. Psalm)
*789 Prepare ye the way (E/G)
*820 When the King shall come again (CT/R)
AK45, 71

Your choice....

Advent 3 *The Lord is very near*
Zephaniah 3:14–18; Isaiah 12:2–6; Phil 4:4–7; LUKE 3:10–18

110 Hail to the Lord's anointed
267 Promised Lord and Christ is he (CT/R)
269 Rejoice in the Lord always (2R)
310 The King of Glory comes (E/G)
405 Awake, awake, fling off the night (E/G)
531 Lest he be too far from us
537 Like a sea without a shore
571 O what a gift(vv 1–4)

585 Praise the Lord, ye heavens, adore him
790 Psallite Domino (E/G)
792 Sing a new song (E/G)
800 The voice of God (CT/R)
806 Be here among us (CT/R)
814 We shall draw water joyfully (cf Resp Ps)
AK24

Your choice....

Advent 4 *Out of you will be born the one who is to rule over Israel*
Micah 5:1–4; Ps 79(80); Hebrews 10:5–10; LUKE 1–38

216 O come, O come Emmanuel (E/G)
301 The coming of our God
382 A sign is seen in heaven
426 Christ is coming to set the captives free
436 Come, Lord Jesus, come Lord, come
437 Come, O divine Messiah
439 Come, thou long-expected Jesus
490 Hail Mary, full of grace
491 Hail Mary, full of grace

492 Hail Mary, mother of our God
725 Awake, awake and greet (E/G)
732 Come Saviour, come (E/G)
*742 For you, O Lord
749 Great is the Lord (CT/R)
810 We have a King who comes
823 You shall go out with joy (CT/R)
AK14, 74

Your choice....

Christmas and the feasts of Christmastide which do not change are to be found under Year A, p.31. The following days have alternative readings for Year B but you should check which ones are actually going to be used.

Holy Family *My dear people, we are already the children of God*
I Sam 1:20–22,24–28; Ps 83(84); I John 3:1–2,21–24; LUKE 2:41–52

137 In the bleak midwinter
147 I wonder as I wander
157 Jesus my Lord, my God, my all
337 Unto us is born a son
382 A sign is seen in heaven
421 Child in the manger
Your choice....

448 Fashion me a people
649 What child is this
658 Would you like to be happy
675 Psalm 83(84) cf Resp Ps
779 O how lovely (cf Resp Ps)
785 One shall tell another
     see also years A and B

The Baptism of The Lord *Here is the Lord coming with power*
Isaiah 40:1–5,9–11; Ps 103(104); Titus 2:11–14; 3:4–7; LUKE 3:15–16,21–22

 16 A voice cries in the wilderness = AK71
110 Hail to the Lord's anointed
242 Open your ears, O Christian people (E/G)
566 O comfort my people (E/G)
596 Send forth your Spirit, O Lord
614 The light of Christ (E/G)
619 The Spirit of God rests upon me
Your choice....

633 To God our Father be the praise (see Tunefinder)
651 When Jesus comes to be baptised
724 All the ends of the earth (E/G)
819 When John baptised
820 When the King shall come
AK24, 71

Lent and Eastertide, Year A

The gospels for Lent 1 and 2 are, as usual, those of Jesus' temptation and his transfiguration; in Luke's versions, naturally. In other years John's Gospel is read for the rest of Lent but Year C continues with Luke. There are two passages on the theme of Repentance (3 – the barren fig tree; 4 – the prodigal Son (repeated on Sunday 24 of Ordinary Time). Sunday 5 is John's story of the woman taken in adultery, a story showing the compassion of Jesus which harmonises well with the spirit of Luke.

As usual, the Lenten Old Testament readings are passage of great importance, such as the 'creed of the chosen people' (Sunday 1) and the covenant of God with Abraham (Sunday 2).

In Eastertide the gospels are as usual from John and the First Readings from Acts. The Second Readings are mostly from the Apocalypse, with its visions of the heavenly triumph of the Lamb.

Ash Wednesday *See Year A, p.34*

Lent 1 *Everyone who calls on the name of the Lord will be saved*
Deuteronomy 26:4–10; Ps 90(91); Rom 10:8–13; LUKE 4:1–13
Rite of Blessing of Water:
Water of life (Eucharist section)
AK1

25	Attend and keep this happy fast (E/G)	635	Trust in the Lord
80	Forty days and forty nights	663	You shall cross the barren desert (CT/R)
81	From the deep I lift my voice	667	Psalm 90 (Resp Ps)
165	Lead us, heavenly Father, lead us	746	God is my great desire
180	Lord Jesus, think on me	*751	Hear us, Almighty Lord (E/G)
183	Lord, who throughout these forty days	778	Oh God, I seek you (E/G)
350	We will walk through the valley	*788	Praise to you, O Christ (Gosp Acc)
362	Yahweh, you are my strength	791	Safe in the shadow (Ps 90/91)
411	Blest be the Lord (cf Resp Ps)		AK1, 3, 20, 21, 27 (cf Resp Ps), *46 (Gosp Acc)

Your choice....

Lent 2 *They saw his glory*
Genesis 15:5–12,17–18; Ps 26(27); Phil 3:17–4:1 (or 3:20–4:1): LUKE 9:28–36

120	Holy Father, God of might (CT/R)	737	Eye has not seen
203	My God, how wonderful thou art	739	Father, we come to you (E/G)
428	Christ is the world's light (CT/R)	748	God, your glory we have seen (CT/R)
560	No one can give to me that peace (Cor)	763	Jesus, lead the way
570	O raise your eyes on high and see	768	Lord, the light of your love
670	Psalm 26(27) Resp Ps	769	Majesty
727	Before the heaven and earth		AK16 (cf Resp Ps), 46

Your choice....

Lent 3 *It is he who forgives all your guilt*
Exodus 3:1–8,13–15; Ps 102(103); I Cor 10:1–6,10–12; LUKE 13:1–9
Day for the First Scrutiny: Year A readings may be used instead

191	Many times I have turned	544	Lord, graciously hear us
223	O God, thy people gather	577	Our Father, we have wandered
227	O Lord my God, when I in awesome wonder	660	You, Israel, return now
228	O holy Lord, by all adored	681	Ps 102(103): Resp Ps
260	Praise, my soul, the King of heaven (cf Resp Ps)	728	Bless the Lord, my soul (cf Resp Ps)
354	When Israel was in Egypt's land	750	Who calls my life again (cf Resp Ps)
457	Fear not, rejoice and be glad	771	My soul cannot be still
477	God forgave my sin in Jesus' name	780	O Lord be not mindful
			AK31 (cf Resp Ps), 46

Lent 4 *This man welcomes sinners*
Joshua 5:9–12; Ps 33(34); 2 Cor 5:17–21; LUKE 15:1–3,11–32
Day for the Second Scrutiny: Year A readings may be used instead

185 Love is his word
191 Many times I have turned (Pen.Rite)
202 My God, and is thy table spread
223 O God, thy people gather (E/G)
249 O thou, who at thy Eucharist (Comm)
297 Take our bread, we ask you (PG)
359 Where would we be without Christ the Lord
385 Across the years (see v3)
477 God forgave my sin in Jesus' name
511 I will never forget you, my people
523 Jesus the Lord said 'I am the bread'

577 Our Father, we have wandered (E/G)
578 Our help is the name of the Lord (E/G)
579 Our Saviour Jesus Christ proclaimed
591 Return to the Lord, return (E/G)
660 You, Israel, return now
754 I received the living God (CT)
758 In the land there is a hunger
770 My people, I hear you calling (E/G)
774 Now in this banquet (Comm)
785 One shall tell another
AK17 (cf Resp Ps), 46, 66

Your choice....

Lent 5 *Go, and don't sin any more*
Isaiah 43:16–21; Ps 125(126); Phil 3:8–14; JOHN 8:1–11
Day for the Third Scrutiny: Year A readings may be used instead
Select hymns from last week, also:

228 O holy Lord, by all adored (PG)
260 Praise my soul the King of Heaven
473 Glory and praise to our God
477 God forgave my sin in Jesus' name
688 Psalm 125(126) (Resp Ps)

728 Bless the Lord, my soul
756 If God should lead us (cf Resp Ps)
803 To God be the glory
813 We're forgiven
AK1, 46

Your choice....

Holy Week and Easter Day
See Year A, p.36

General Eastertide: *See p. 39*

Easter 2 *Happy are those who have not seen and yet believe*
Acts 5:12–16; Ps 117(118); Apoc 1:9–13,17–19; JOHN 20:19–31

56 Crown him with many crowns (v3: Gosp)
95 Godhead here in hiding (v.4: Gosp)
302 The day of resurrection
364 Ye sons and daughters (vv.8–9)
433 Come, God's people (E/G)
493 He is Lord

735 Confitemini Domino (cf Resp Ps) (E/G)
756 If God should lead us (CT/R)
762 Jesus is Lord (CT/R)
815 We walk by faith
AK33 (cf Resp Ps), 47

Your choice....

81

Easter 3 *Feed my sheep. Follow me.*
Acts 5:27–32,40,41; Psalm 29(30); Apoc 5:11–14; JOHN 21:1–19 (or 1–14)

395 Alleluia, alleluia, give thanks
445 'Do you really love me?'
458 'Feed my lambs, my son'
460 Follow me, follow me
510 I will be with you
626 This is the feast of victory (2R)

744 Forth in the peace (CT/R)
794 Sing of the Lord's goodness
795 Sing it in the valleys (CT/R)
809 We have a gospel to proclaim (CT/R)
818 What is this place (E/G)

Your choice....

Easter 4 *We are his people, the sheep of his flock*
Acts 13:14,43–52; Ps 99(100); Apoc 7:9,14–17; JOHN 10:27–30

 10 All people that on earth (cf Resp Ps) (E/G)
187 Loving shepherd of thy sheep
311 The King of love my shepherd is
312 The Lord's my shepherd, I'll not want
387 Alabare (cf 2R)
390 All the earth proclaim the Lord (cf Resp Ps) (E/G)
494 He is risen, alleluia

565 O be joyful in the Lord
586 Praise to the Lord! Praise him
615 The Lord is my shepherd
680 Psalm 99(100) (Resp Ps)
731 Come, rejoice (cf Resp Ps) (E/G)
745 Free as is the morning sun
793 Sing, all creation (cf Resp Ps) (E/G)
AK30 (cf Resp Ps), 66

Your choice....

Easter 5 *How good is the Lord to all, compassionate to all his creatures*
Acts 14:21–27; Ps 144(145); Apoc 21:1–5; JOHN 13:31–35

139 Into one we all are gathered
327 This is my will, my one command
358 Where is love and loving-kindness
380 A new commandment
489 Greater love has no man
576 One day will come (cf.2R)
628 This is what Yahweh asks of you

691 Psalm 144(145) (Resp Ps)
730 Christ triumphant
734 Come we that love the Lord (2R)
748 God, your glory we have seen (CT/R)
761 It is good to give thanks (E/G)
AK38 (cf Resp Ps), 66

Your choice....

Easter 6 *A peace the world cannot give*
Acts 15:1–2,22–29; Ps 66(67); Apoc 21:10–14,22–23; JOHN 14:23–29

255 Peace is the gift
257 Peace, perfect peace
384 Abba, Father (see v.7)
502 I am the vine
553 May the peace of the Lord
558 My soul is longing for your peace
560 No one can give to me that peace

581 Peace is my parting gift
628 This is what Yahweh asks of you
632 To be the body of the Lord
786 Peace I give
811 We have been told
825 You are the vine = AK67

Your choice....

82

Ascension *Jesus at the right hand of God*
Acts 1:1–11; Ps 46(47); Hebrews 9:24–28; 10:19–23; LUKE 24:46–53

7 Alleluia, sing to Jesus
28 At the name of Jesus
108 Hail the day that sees him rise
207 New praises be given
270 Rejoice! the Lord is King!
308 The head that once was crowned
429 Christ is the world's redeemer (see Tunefinder)
493 He is Lord

510 I will be with you
525 Jesus, you are Lord
714 Stand and stare not (round) (CT/R)
727 Before the heaven and earth
730 Christ triunphant
748 God, your glory we have seen (CT/R)
762 Jesus is Lord (CT/R)
AK31 (cf Resp Ps)

Your choice....

Easter 7 *He saw the glory of God and Jesus standing at his right hand*
Acts 7:55–56; Psalm 96(97); Apoc 22:12–14,16–17,20; JOHN 17:20–26

As ascension; also
249 O thou, who at thy Eucharist (CT)
363 Ye choirs of new Jerusalem (E/G)
383 Abba, abba Father (v2 cf Gosp)
470 Give praise to the Lord (E/G)

594 Send forth your Spirit, God our Father (1–4)
762 Jesus is Lord (CT/R)
804 To Jesus Christ, our sovereign King (CT/R)
809 We have a Gospel to proclaim (CT/R)
824 You are the King of glory

Your choice....

Pentecost *Send forth your Spirit, O Lord*

37 Breath on me, breath of God
49 Come down, O love divine
50 Come, holy Ghost
99 God's Spirit is in my heart
124 Holy Spirit, Lord of light (Sequence)
125 Holy Spirit of fire
225 Oh living water
289 Spirit of the living God
342 We are one in the Spirit
384 Abba, Father, send your spirit
393 Alleluia, may God's Spirit come
453 Father, Lord of all creation
485 God's Spirit precedes us

460 Follow me
595/6 Send forth your Spirit (cf Resp Ps)
617 The Spirit is moving
619 The Spirit of God rests upon me
625 This is the day
638 Veni, sancte Spiritus (E/G)
657 Wind and fire
682 Psalm 103 (104): Resp. Psalm
700 Breath of life (round)
720 Veni creator Spiritus (E/G)
744 Forth in the peace of Christ (CT/R)
797 The gift of the Holy Spirit (CT/R)
AK32 (cf Resp Ps), 44 (Gosp Acc)

Your choice....

Trinity *The Spirit of truth will glorify me: everything the Father has is mine*
Proverbs 8:22–31; Psalm 8; Rom 5:1–5; JOHN 16:12–15

70 Father most holy
75 Firmly I believe and truly
121 Holy God, we praise thy name (E/G)
122/3 Holy, holy, holy (E/G)

130 I believe in God the Father
165 Lead us, heavenly Father
194 Merrily on
198 Most ancient of all mysteries

282 Sing people of God (cf Resp Ps)
284 Sing praises to the living God
451 Father in heaven
452 Father, in my life
453 Father, Lord of all creation (CT/R)
455 Father, we praise you, now the night is over
459 Firm is our faith

509 I was born before creation (1R)
629 Thou whose almighty Word (E/G)
665 Psalm 8: Resp Ps
702 Glory be to God the Father (round)
740 For call to faith
768 Lord, the light of your love (CT/R)
AK85

Your choice....

The Body and Blood of Christ (Corpus Christi)

Anyone who eats this bread will live for ever
Genesis 14:18–20; Ps 109(110); I Cor 11:23–26; LUKE 9:11–17

7 Alleluia, sing to Jesus
65 Draw nigh and take (Comm)
135 In bread we bring you (PG)
166 Let all mortal flesh (PG)
177 Lord, accept the gifts (PG)
185 Love is his word
202 My God, and is thy table spread
249 O thou who at thy Eucharist (CT)
264 Praise to the Lord, the Almighty (PG)
324 They say I am wise
344 We celebrate this festive day (E/G)
399 An upper room
402 As long as men on earth
403 As one body (Comm)
408 Before Christ died (see Tunefinder)
412 Bread of the world (for choir use?)
438 Come, O Lord, to my heart
501 I am the bread of life
521 Jesus said 'I am the bread'

523 Jesus the Lord said 'I am the bread'
543 Lord enthroned in heavenly splendour (CT/R)
567 O food of travellers
597 Shepherd of souls
623 This is my body
637 Upon thy table, Lord (PG)
643 We form one Church (CT/R)
648 Welcome, all ye noble saints
653 When the time came
764 Jesus, Lord of life and love
765 Jesus, you're the one I love
774 Now in this banquet (Comm/CT)
787 Praise now your God (CT/R)
802 Those who were in the dark
818 What is this place (E/G)
Eucharist section: Lamb of God 2–4
Psalm 109(110) (Resp Ps) is to be found in Evening Prayer
AK51, 66, 68, 69

Your choice....

Sacred Heart *I have found my sheep that was lost*
Ezekiel 34:11–16; Ps 22(23); Romans 5:5–11; LUKE 15:3–7

★ Versions of Ps 22(23)
15 All ye who seek a comfort sure
97 God is love, his the care
150 Jesu, lover of my soul
161 King of glory, King of peace
248 O Sacred Heart
260 Praise, my soul (cf Resp Ps)
288 Soul of my Saviour
293 Sweet heart of Jesus
★311 The King of love

★312 The Lord's my shepherd
334 To Jesus' heart all-burning
499 His light now shines
★615 The Lord is my shepherd
★667 Psalm 22(23)
696 Adoramus te, Domine
728 Bless the Lord, my soul (cf Resp Ps)
765 Jesus, you're the one I love = AK 69
★777 O Christe Domine Jesu
AK13 (cf Resp Ps), 77, 81

Your choice....

Ordinary Time, Year C

YEAR C is the Year of Luke. Luke's Gospel is often known as the Gospel of Compassion because of the frequent signs of Jesus' mercy and compassion which it contains, most strikingly, perhaps, the Prodigal Son (24th Sunday). But there is also the Centurion's servant (9th Sunday), the son of the Widow of Nain (10th Sunday), the Good Samaritan (15th), Zacchaeus (31st) and many other examples. Notice two familiar prayers in versions different from what we are used to: the Beatitudes (6th Sun) and the Lord's Prayer (17th).

Much of the Gospel is set in the context of Jesus' journey to Jerusalem. This begins on the 13th Sunday, after Jesus has finished his Galilean Ministry (chapters 5 to 9 of the Gospel) and a week after the acknowledgement by Peter of the Messiahship of Jesus. This journey is not to be taken just as a trip from A to B but as an image of the journey we all make with Jesus to his inevitable death and his glorious resurrection. It is in these chapters that Luke collects most of the material that is special to his Gospel.

The year ends on the 34th Sunday with another story which is special to Luke, when Jesus on the cross promises that the repentant thief will be with him that day in paradise.

NOTES

1. Asterisked hymns may be used on more than one Sunday in a particular season.
2. Some hymns are based on one or other of the Readings of the day and these are noted as follows: 1R = First Reading; 2R = Second Reading; Gosp = Gospel;
3. Suggestions for the use of the hymns at Mass are noted thus (note that these are *suggestions* only): E/G = Entrance/Gathering; PG = Preparation of Gifts; Comm = Communion; R = Recessional, CT/R = Communion Thanksgiving or Recessional.
4. If you need EXTRA HYMNS: see p.27
5. Learning NEW HYMNS: see p.24
6. Space is provided after each Sunday for your own choice of hymns. Good ideas should be written down straight away so they are not forgotten.

Sunday 2 *A wedding at Cana: Jesus let his glory be seen*
Isaiah 62:1–5; Ps 95(96); I Cor 12:4–11; JOHN 2:1–11

58	Day by day in the market place	496	He's a most unusual man
65	Draw nigh and take the body of the Lord	567	O food of travellers
69	Father and life-giver	648	Welcome all you noble saints
110	Hail to the Lord's anointed	772	New songs of celebration
264	Praise to the Lord, the almighty	774	Now in this banquet (Comm/CT)
280	Sing of the bride and sing of the groom	785	One shall tell another
286	Songs of thankfulness and praise	787	Praise now your God (CT/R)
344	We celebrate this festive day (E/G)	790	Psallite Domino (E/G)
408	Before Christ died (E/G)	818	What is this place (E/G)
469	Gifts of bread and wine (PG)		

Your choice....

Sunday 3 *This text is being fulfilled today even as you listen*

Nehemiah 8:2–6,8–10; Ps 18(19); I Cor 12:12–30 (or 12–14,27); LUKE 1:1–4; 4:14–21

43	Christ is our King	619	The Spirit of God rests upon me
45	Colours of day	666	Psalm 18(19) (Resp Ps)
99	God's spirit is in my heart	747	God who spoke in the beginning
110	Hail to the Lord's anointed	788	Praise to you, O Christ our Saviour
242	Open your ears, O Christian people	798	The kingdom of God (CT/R)
319	The spirit of the Lord	799	The master came to bring good news (CT/R)
496	He's a most unusual man	800	The voice of God (CT/R)
500	Our God reigns	801	The word of God = AK11 (cf Resp Ps)
614	The light of Christ (E/G)		

Your choice....

Sunday 4 *I have appointed you prophet. No prophet is accepted in his own country*

Jeremiah 1:4–5,17–19; Ps 70(71); I Cor 12:31–13:13 (or 13:4–13); LUKE 4:21–30

16	A voice cries in the wilderness = AK71	526	Keep in mind (2R)
64	Do you know that the Lord walks on earth	531	Lest he be too far from us
86	Glorious God, King of creation	574	Oh the word of my Lord
102	Go, the Mass is ended	753	How shall they hear the word of God
139	Into one we all are gathered	781	O Lord, you are the centre
184	Love divine, all loves excelling	782	O most high and glorious God (2R)
310	The king of glory comes	791	Safe in the shadow
324	They say I am wise		AK71, 83 (2R)
340	Walk with me, O my Lord		

Your choice....

Sunday 5 *I am a sinful man, Lord.*
Do not be afraid; you will be a fisher of men

Isaiah 6:1–8; Psalm 137(138); I Cor 15:1–11 (or 15:3–8,11)

Point out connection of 1st reading with Holy, Holy

60	Dear Lord and Father of mankind	496	He's a most unusual man
78/744	Forth in the peace of Christ (CT/R)	508	I the Lord of sea and sky
79	Forth in thy name, O Lord (CT/R)	530	Leave your country and your people
119	He who would valiant be	542	Lord, confronted with your might
122	Holy holy (E/G)	545	Lord, in everything I do (PG)
123	Holy, holy, holy, Lord God almighty (E/G)	550	Lord, you have come to the lakeside
296	Take my hands (PG)	607	Son of the Father
325	This day God gives me	608	Take my life and let it be
351	What can we offer you	753	How shall they hear the Word
444	Do not be afraid	797	The gift of the Holy Spirit (CT/R)
449	Father, hear the prayer we offer	818	What do you want of me, Lord
460	Follow me, follow me		AK37 (cf Resp Ps), 76

Your choice....

Sunday 6 *Happy are those who place their trust in the Lord*
Jeremiah 17:5–8; Psalm 1; I Cor 15:12,16–20; LUKE 6:17,20–26

6 Alleluia! I will praise the Father	417 But I say unto you
32 Be still and know I am with you	663 You shall cross the barren desert
35 Be thou my vision	696 The Beatitudes
36 Blest are the pure in heart	726 As a tree planted
111 Happy the man	754 I received the living God
317 There is a world	775 O changeless Christ
320 The Kingdom = AK73	817 What does the Lord require
336 Trust is in the eyes of a tiny babe	AK73
350 We will walk through the shadow	

Your choice....

Sunday 7 *Treat others as you would like them to treat you*
I Sam 26:2,7–9,12–13,22–23; Ps 102(103); I Cor 15:45–49; LUKE 6:27–38

s1 God gives his people strength	612 The Church is wherever
139 Into one we all are gathered	636 Unite us, Lord, in peace
178 Lord, for tomorrow and its needs	656 Who wants to live as God
260 Praise, my soul, the King of Heaven	681 Psalm 102(103) (Resp Ps)
317 There is a world	728 Bless the Lord, my soul (cf Resp Ps) (E/G)
327 This is my will, my one command	750 Who calls my life again (cf Resp Ps)
334 To Jesus' heart all-burning	782 O most high and glorious God
338 Vaster far than any ocean	799 The Master came to bring good news (CT/R)
358 Where is love and loving kindness	807 We are your people (CT/R)
417 But I say unto you	808 We give God thanks (CT/R)
477 God forgave my sin	AK31 (cf Resp Ps)
499 His light now shines in the darkness	

Your choice....

Sunday 8 *By their fruits you shall know them*
Ecclus 27:4–7; Ps 91(92); I Cor 15:54–58; LUKE 6:39–45

s7 Lord, make me an instrument of thy peace	320 The kingdom
35 Be thou my vision	397 Almighty Father, who for us
36 Blest are the pure of heart	497 Help us accept each other
37 Breathe on me, breath of God	520 It's good to give thanks (cf Resp Ps)
111 Happy the man	537 Like a sea without a shore (2R)
165 Lead us, heavenly Father, lead us	593 Seek ye first
189 Make me a channel of your peace	726 As a tree planted
191 Many times I have turned	759 In the Lord I'll be ever thankful (E/G, Comm)
201 My God, accept my heart (PG)	
296 Take my hands (PG)	761 It is good to give thanks (cf Resp Ps) (E/G)
297 Take our bread (PG)	781 Centre of my life

Your choice....

Sunday 9 *Proclaim the Good News*
I Kings 8:41–43; Ps 116(117); Gal 1:1–2,6–10; LUKE 7:1–10

9	All hail the power of Jesus' name	661	You must cry out the word of the Lord
14	All this world belongs to Jesus	664	The eyes of the blind
43	Christ is our King	685	Psalm 116 (117) (Resp Ps)
45	Colours of day	703	(round) Go out to the whole world
53	Come, praise the Lord (cf Resp Ps)	708	(round) Let us go forth
78	Forth in the peace of Christ (also 744) (CT/R)	785	One shall tell another
79	Forth in thy name (CT/R)	798	The Kingdom of God
102	Go, the Mass is ended	799	The Master came (CT/R)
136	In Christ there is no East nor West	803	To God be the glory (CT/R)
390	All the earth proclaim the Lord (E/G)	809	We have a Gospel to proclaim (CT/R)
391	All you nations	815	We walk by faith
447	Faith in God can move the mountains	AK6	
605	Sing to the world of Christ		

Your choice....

Sunday 10 *O Lord, you have raised my soul from the dead*
I Kings 17:17–24; Ps 29(30); Gal 1:11–19; LUKE 7:11–17

7	Alleluia, sing to Jesus	528	Lay your hands gently upon us
15	All ye who seek a comfort sure	618	Walk in the light
94	God everlasting, wonderful and holy	750	Who calls my life again
222	O God, our help in ages past	774	Now in this banquet
266	Praise we our God with joy	775	O changeless Christ
345	We gather together	795	Sing it in the valleys
386	Again the Lord's own day is here	824	You are the King of glory
405	Awake, awake, fling off the night	AK10	
447	Faith in God can move the mountains		

Your choice....

Sunday 11 *The one who is forgiven much, shows much love*
2 Sam 12:7–10,13; Ps 31(1–2,5,7,11)

Rite of Blessing of Water:
Water of Life (Eucharist Section), AK1

757	In the abundance of your compassion	454	Father of heaven, whose love (E/G)
		455	Father, we praise you (E/G)
		477	God forgave my sin
19	Amazing grace!	544	Lord, graciously hear us
81	From the deep I lift my voice	577	Our Father, we have wandered (E/G)
150	Jesus, lover of my soul	743	Forgive our sins as we forgive
158	Jesus! thou art coming	751	Hear us almighty Lord (E/G)
178	Lord, for tomorrow	764	Jesus, Lord of life and love
191	Many times I have turned	780	O Lord, be not mindful (Pen.Rite)
223	O God, thy people gather (E/G)	794	Sing of the Lord's goodness (CT/R)
385	Across the years there echoes still	813	We're forgiven
447	Faith in God can move the mountains (2R)	AK1, 20	

Your choice....

Sunday 12 *Who do you say I am? Peter spoke up: The Christ of God.*
Zech 12:10–11; 13:1; Ps62(63); Gal 3:26–29; LUKE 9:18–24

28	At the name of Jesus	449	Father, hear the prayer we offer
75	Firmly I believe and truly	506	I met you at the cross
88	Glory be to Jesus	508	Here I am, Lord
130	I believe in God the Father	526	Keep in mind
156	Jesus, Lord, I'll sing a song	528	Like the deer that thirsts
179	Lord Jesus Christ	656	Who wants to live as God
201	My God accept my heart	674	Ps 62(32) (Resp Ps)
224	O God, we give ourselves	730	Christ triumphant
324	They say I am wise	746	God is my great desire
355	When I survey	762	Jesus is Lord (CT/R)
418	By his wounds	778	Oh God, I seek you (cf Resp Ps)
428	Christ is the world's light	812	Unless a grain of wheat (Comm/CT)
429	Christ is the world's redeemer	AK22	(cf Resp Ps)

Your choice...

Sunday 13 *No one who looks back is fit for the kingdom*
I Kings 19:16,19–21; Ps 15(16); Gal 5:1,13–18; LUKE 9:51–62
Jesus' journey to Jerusalem begins: see p.85.

73	Fight the good fight	449	Father, hear the prayer we offer
74	Fill my house	460	Follow me, follow me
76	Follow Christ and love the world	510	I will be with you
78/744	Forth in thy name (CT/R)	530	Leave your country and your people
102	Go, the Mass is ended	545	Lord, in everything I do (PG)
104	Guide me, O thou great redeemer (CT/R)	547	Lord of creation (PG)
119	He who would valiant be	634	Together we journey
197	Moses, I know you're the man	781	Centre of my life (cf Resp Ps)
296	Take my hands	797	The gift of the Holy Spirit (CT/R)
313	The Mass is ended, all go in peace	816	What do you want of me
331	Thy hand, O God, has guided	AK76	
350	We will walk through the valley		

Your choice....

Sunday 14 *Go out and say: Peace be to this house. The Kingdom is very near to you*
Isaiah 66:10–14; Ps 65(66); Gal 6:14–18; LUKE 10:1–12,17–20 (or 10:1–9)

79	Forth in thy name, O Lord (CT/R)	605	Sing to the world of Christ (CT/R)
253	O worship the king	612	The Church is wherever
254	Peace is flowing like a river (1R)	701	Dona nobis pacem (round)
255	Peace is the gift	707	Jubilate Deo (E/G)
257	Peace, perfect peace	731	Come, rejoice before your maker (E/G)
355	When I survey (2R)	744	Forth in the peace (R)
391	All you nations (cf Resp Ps) (E/G)	761	It is good to give thanks (E/G)
467	Gather, Christians (E/G)	772	New songs of celebration
474	Glory to God	785	One shall tell another
500	Our God reigns	798	The kingdom of God
553	May the peace of the Lord	809	We have a gospel to proclaim (CT/R)
593	Seek ye first the kingdom of God	AK23	

Your choice....

Sunday 15 *You must love the Lord your God... and your neighbour as yourself*
Deut 30:10–14; Ps 68(69) or 18(19); Col 1:15–20; LUKE 10:25–37

96	God is love	376	A certain traveller (Gosp)
97	God is love, his the care	380	A new commandment
136	In Christ there is no east or west	417	But I say unto you
139	Into one we all are gathered	453	Father, Lord of all creation
189	Make me a channel of your peace	612	The Church is wherever
210	Now Jesus said 'You must love one another'	666	Psalm 18(19) (Resp Ps)
317	There is a world where people come and go	797	The gift of the Holy Spirit
327	This is my will, my one command	801	The word of God (cf Resp Ps) = AK11
342	We are one in the Spirit	807	We are your people
352	Whatsoever you do	817	What does the Lord require
358	Where is love and loving-kindness	AK11	

Your choice....

Sunday 16 *Abraham welcomes the Lord; Martha welcomes Jesus*
Genesis 18:1–10; Ps 14(15); Col 1:24–28; LUKE 10:38–42

10	All people that on earth do dwell	524	Jesus the Lord has lived among us
32	Be still and know	531	Lest he be too far from us
36	Blest are the pure in heart	537	Like a sea without a shore
41	Christ be beside me	668	Psalm 23 (24)
152	Jesu, the very thought of thee	670	One thing I ask of the Lord (Ps 26)
181	Lord of all hopefulness	746	God is my great desire
231	Oh the love of my Lord	754	I received the living God (CT)
237	O my Lord, within my heart	763	Jesus, lead the way
404	As the bridegroom to his chosen	764	Jesus, Lord of life and love
435	Come, let us sing out our joy	781	Centre of my life
438	Come, O Lord, to my heart today	806	Be here among us (CT/R)
441	Day by day, dear Lord	818	What is this place (E/G)
471	Give us the will to listen		

Your choice....

Sunday 17 *Lord, teach us to pray... Ask and you will receive*
Genesis 18:2–32; Ps 137(138); Col 2:12–14; LUKE 11:1–13

15	All ye who seek a comfort sure	450	Father I place into your hands (PG)
17	Almighty Father, Lord most high (PG)	451	Father in heaven
23	Ask, and you will receive	473	Glory and praise to our God
63	Do not worry over what to eat	481	God made the birds
85	Give me yourself, O Jesus Christ	501	I am the bread of life
94	God everlasting, merciful and holy	523	Jesus the Lord said
155	Jesus, Lord, I'll sing (Gosp)	579	Our Saviour Jesus Christ proclaimed
165	Lead us, heavenly Father	739	Father, we come to you (E/G)
171	Let us with a gladsome mind	754	I received the living God (CT)
249	O thou who at thy eucharist (CT)	758	In the land there is a hunger
264	Praise to the Lord, the almighty (PG)	794	Sing of the Lord's goodness (CT/R)
415	Bright star of morning	AK37 (cf Resp Ps)	

Your choice....

Sunday 18 *Do not store up treasure for yourself on earth*
Eccles 1:2; 2:21–23; Ps 89(90) or 94(95); Col 3:1–5,9–11; LUKE 12:13–21

35	Be thou my vision	435	Come, let us sing out ((cf Resp Ps 2)
36	Blest are the pure in heart	517	In God alone is there rest for my soul
49	Come down, O love divine	525	Jesus, you are Lord
60	Dear Lord and Father of mankind	558	My soul is longing for your peace
63	Do not worry over what to eat	608	Take my life and let it be
134	Immortal, invisible	679	Psalm 94 (95) (Resp Ps 2)
166	Let all mortal flesh keep silence (PG)	737	Eye has not seen (CT)
201	My God, accept my heart (PG)	758	In the Land there is a hunger
222	O God, our help in ages past (cf Resp Ps 1)	763	Jesus, lead the way
226	Oh Lord, all the world belongs to you	774	Now in this banquet (Comm/CT)
237	Oh my Lord, within my heart	783	O that today = AK28 (cf Resp Ps 2)
389	All my hope on God is founded		AK26 (cf Resp Ps 1), 28 (cf Resp Ps 2)
402	As long as men on earth		

Your choice....

Sunday 19 *Happy the people the Lord has chosen as his own*
Wis 18:6–9; Psalm 32(33); Heb 11:1–2,8–19 (or 1–2,8–12); LUKE 12:32–48 (or 35–40)

10	All people that on earth do dwell (E/G)	448	Fashion me a people
45	Colours of day	456	Fear not, for I have redeemed you
181	Lord of all hopefulness	463	For to those who love God
184	Love divine, all loves excelling	530	Leave your country (cf 2R)
227	O Lord my God, when I in awesome wonder	545	Lord, in everything I do (PG)
233	O Jesus Christ remember	550	Lord, you have come to the lakeside
267	Promised Lord and Christ is he	588	Rejoice and shout for joy (cf Resp Ps) (E/G)
300	The Church's one foundation	643	We form one Church, one Christian folk
350	We will walk through the valley	728	Bless the Lord, my soul (E/G)
362	Yahweh, you are my strength	793	Sing, all creation (E/G)
390	All the earth, proclaim the Lord	807	We are your people
405	Awake, awake, fling off the night	822	You are the Lord
441	Day by day dear Lord		

Your choice....

Sunday 20 *God's word can make people take sides*
Jer 38:4–6,8–10; Ps 39(40); Heb 12:1–4; LUKE 12:49–53

s1	God gives his people strength	456	Fear not, for I have redeemed you
15	All ye who seek a comfort sure	463	For to those who love God
104	Guide me, O thou great Redeemer (CT/R)	485	God's Spirit precedes us
150	Jesu, lover of my soul	504/5	I lift (up) my eyes
151	Jesu, meek and lowly	526	Keep in mind
164	Lead, kindly light	549	Lord, thy word abideth
165	Lead us, heavenly Father, lead us	605	Sing to the world (CT/R)
221	O God of earth and altar (E/G)	649	We gather together (E/G)
362	Yahweh you are my strength	739	Father we come to you (E/G)
407	Be still, my soul	759	In the Lord (Comm)
444	Do not be afraid	767	Lead us from death to life (CT/R)
449	Father, hear the prayer we offer	773	Nothing can ever take away
452	Father, in my life I see		AK34

Your choice....

Sunday 21 *I am coming to gather the nations into the kingdom*
Isaiah 66:18–21; Ps 116(117); Heb 12:5–7,11–13; LUKE 13:22–30

7	Alleluia! sing to Jesus	523	Jesus the Lord said
45	Colours of day	597	Shepherd of souls (CT/R)
53	Come, praise the Lord (cf Resp Ps) (PG)	609	Tell out, my soul (CT/R)
136	In Christ there is no east or west	648	Welcome all ye noble saints (PG)
139	Into one we all are gathered	685	Psalm 116 (117) (Resp Ps)
202	My God, and is thy table spread	703	Go out to the whole world (round)
331	Thy hand, O God, has guided	752	Gather us in (E/G)
344	We celebrate this festive day (E/G)	774	Now in this banquet (Comm/CT)
345	We gather together (E/G)	785	One shall tell another
435	Come, let us sing out our joy (E/G)	798	The kingdom of God

Your choice....

Sunday 22 *The one who humbles himself will be exalted*
Ecclus 3:17–20,28–29; Ps 67(68); Heb 12:18–19,22–24; LUKE 14:1,7–14

6	Alleluia! I will praise the Father	287	Sons of God
35	Be thou my vision	399	An upper room
36	Blest are the pure in heart	462	For the healing of the nations
43	Christ is our King	535	Let us talents and tongues
54	Come to the Lord	558	My soul is longing
72	Feed us now	612	The church is wherever
185	Love is his word	648	Welcome all ye noble saints
186	Loving Father, from thy bounty (PG)	736	As a tree planted
190	Man of Galilee	752	Gather us in (E/G)
275	See us, Lord, about thine altar (CT)	807	We are your people

Your choice....

Sunday 23 *Who can divine the will of the Lord?*
'Anyone who does not carry his cross cannot be my disciple'
Wisdom 9:13–18; Ps 89(90); Philemon 9–10,12–17; LUKE 14:25–33

s1	God gives his people strength	488	Grant us thy peace
11	All that I am	506	I met you at the cross
35	Be thou my vision	526	Keep in mind
37	Breathe on me, breath of God	550	Lord, you have come to the lakeside
73	Fight the good fight	598	Show me your ways (CT/R)
222	O God, our help in ages past (cf Resp Ps)	656	Who wants to live as God
355	When I survey	767	Lead us from death to life (CT/R)
389	All my hope in God is founded (E/G)	782	O most high and gracious God
449	Father, hear the prayer we offer	812	Unless a grain of wheat (Comm/CT)
460	Follow me (CT/R)	AK26	(cf Resp Ps)

Your choice....

Sunday 24 *This son of mine was dead and has come back to life*
Exodus 32:7–11,13–14; Ps 50(51); I Tim 1:12–17; LUKE 15:1–32 (or 1–10) – The Prodigal Son

19 Amazing grace	577 Our Father, we have wandered (E/G)
70 Father most holy, merciful and loving	591 Return to the Lord, return (E/G)
191 Many times I have turned (Pen.Rite)	648 Welcome all ye noble saints (PG)
223 O God, thy people gather (E/G)	660 You Israel return now
228 O holy Lord, by all adored (PG)	673 Psalm 50(51) (cf Resp Ps)
231 Oh, the love of my Lord	728 Bless the Lord, my soul (E/G)
260 Praise, my soul	739 Father, we come to you (E/G)
266 Praise we our God with joy	743 Forgive our sins as we forgive
338 Vaster far than any ocean	750 Who calls my life again
385 Across the years there echoes still	770 My people, I hear you calling (E/G)
454 Father of heaven, whose love profound (E/G)	780 O Lord, be not mindful of our sins (Pen.Rite)
477 God forgave my sin (CT/R)	794 Sing of the Lord's goodness
	AK1, 20 (cf Resp Ps)

Sunday 25 *If you cannot be trusted with money, that tainted thing, who will trust you with genuine riches?*
Amos 8:4–7; Ps 112(113); I Tim 2:1–8; LUKE 16:1–13 (or 10–13)

35 Be thou my vision	593 Seek ye first the kingdom (E/G)
63 Do not worry over what to eat	609 Tell out my soul (CT/R)
111 Happy the man who wanders	636 Unite us, Lord, in peace
171 Let us, with a gladsome mind (CT/R)	662 You servants of God (cf Resp Ps)
226 Oh Lord, all the world	743 Forgive our sins
397 Almighty Father, who for us	782 O most high and glorious God
417 But I say unto you	797 The gift of the holy Spirit (CT/R)
461 For the fruits of his creation (CT/R)	798 The kingdom of God (CT/R)
462 For the healing of the nations	799 The master came (CT/R)
470 Give praise to the Lord (cf Resp Ps) (E/G)	817 What does the Lord require
591 Return to the Lord, return (E/G)	Psalm 112(113) may be found in Evening Prayer

Your choice....

Sunday 26 *It is the Lord who keeps faith for ever, who is just to those who are oppressed*
Amos 6:1,4–7; Ps 145(146); I Tim 6:11–16; LUKE 16:19–31

6 Alleluia! I will praise the Father (cf Resp Ps) (E/G)	353 When I needed a neighbour
	462 For the healing of the nations
72 Feed us now	612 The church is wherever
76 Follow Christ and love the world (CT/R)	628 This is what Yahweh asks
134 Immortal, invisible (2R) (E/G)	798 The kingdom of God
226 Oh Lord, all the world	799 The master came
237 O my Lord, within my heart	800 The voice of God
312 The Lord's my shepherd	807 We are your people
314 The prophet in his hunger	817 What does the Lord require
345 We gather together as brothers (E/G)	AK39 (cf Resp Ps)

Your choice....

Sunday 27 *We are servants; we have done no more than our duty*
Hab 1:2–3; 2:2–4; Ps 94(95); 2 Tim 1:6–8,13–14; LUKE 17:5–10

s1 God gives his people strength
121 Holy God, we praise thy name (E/G)
164 Lead, kindly light
296 Take my hands
340 Walk with me, O my Lord
362 Yahweh, you are my strength
435 Come, let us sing out our joy (cf Resp Ps)
447 Faith in God can move the mountains
449 Father, hear the prayer we offer
545 Lord, in everything I do (PG)

547 Lord of creation (PG)
550 Lord, you have come to the lakeside
647 We thank you, Father, for the gift
679 Psalm 94(95): Resp Ps
760 In your love remember me = AK15
783 O that today (cf Resp Ps) = AK28
793 Sing. all creation (PG)
816 What do you want of me, Lord?
AK15, 28

Your choice....

Sunday 28 *Finding himself cured, one of them praised God at the top of his voice*
2 Kings 5:14–17; Ps 97(98); 2 Tim 2:8–13; LUKE 17:11–19

19 Amazing grace!
94 God everlasting, wonderful and holy
171 Let us, with a gladsome mind
211 Now thank we all our God (CT/R)
244 O praise ye the Lord (CT/R)
260 Praise, my soul
264 Praise to the Lord, the Almighty (PG)
269 Rejoice in the Lord always (E/G)
283 Sing praises to God
284 Sing praises to the living God

512 I will sing, I will sing (CT/R)
526 Keep in mind (2R) (CT)
585 Praise the Lord! Ye heavens, adore him (E/G)
724 All the ends of the earth (cf Resp Ps) (E/G)
728 Bless the Lord, my soul
735 Confitemini Domino (Comm)
772 New Songs of celebration (cf Resp Ps) (E/G)
792 Sing a new song (cf Resp Ps) (E/G)
794 Sing of the Lord's goodness (CT/R)
AK29 (cf Resp Ps)

Your choice....

Sunday 29 *God will see justice done for those who call to him*
Exodus 17:8–13; Ps 120(121); 2 Tim 3:14–4:2; LUKE 18:1–8

s1 God gives his people strength
15 All ye that seek a comfort sure
23 Ask, and you will receive
130 I believe in God the Father
178 Lord, for tomorrow and its needs
200 My glory, and the lifter of my head
222 O God, our help in ages past
362 Yahweh, you are my strength
389 All my hope on God is founded

504/505 I lift (up) my eyes (cf Resp Ps)
578 Our help is the name of the Lord (E/G)
579 Our Saviour Jesus Christ proclaimed
598 Show me your ways
630 Though the mountains may fall
635 Trust in the Lord
759 In the Lord is my true salvation (E/G, Comm)
AK34 (cf Resp Ps)

Your choice....

Sunday 30 *The one who humbles himself will be exalted*
Ecclus 35:12–14,16–19; Ps 33(34); 2 Tim 4:6–8,16–18

144 It's me, O Lord
150 Jesu, lover of my soul
158 Jesus! thou art coming
191 Many times I have turned
223 O God, thy people gather (E/G)
237 O my Lord, within my heart
338 Vaster far than any ocean
428 Christ is the world's light (CT/R)
Your choice....

450 Father, I place into your hands (PG)
454 Father of heaven, whose love profound (E/G)
577 Our Father, we have wandered (E/G)
711 Ostende nobis, Domine (E/G)
743 Forgive our sins as we forgive
799 The master came to give good news (CT/R)
AK17 (cf Resp Ps)

Sunday 31 *The Son of Man has come to seek out and save what was lost*
Wisdom 11:22–12:2; Ps 144(145); 2 Thess 1:11–2:2; LUKE 19:1–10

11 All that I am
19 Amazing grace
42 Christ is king of earth and heaven
201 My God, accept my heart (PG)
260 Praise, my soul, the King of heaven (E/G)
266 Praise we our God with joy
296 Take my hands (PG)
477 God forgave my sin
Your choice....

630 Though the mountains may fall
691 Ps 144(145) (Resp Ps)
794 Sing of the Lord's goodness (CT/R)
798 The kingdom of God (CT/R)
803 To God be the glory (CT/R)
813 We're forgiven
AK338 (cf Resp Ps)

Sunday 32 *God not of the dead, but of the living*
2 Macc 7:1–2,9–14; Ps 16(17); 2 Thess 2:16–3:5; LUKE 20:27–38 (or 27.34–38)

128 I am the bread of life
164 Lead, kindly light
184 Love divine, all loves excelling
187 Loving shepherd of thy sheep
288 Soul of my Saviour
300 The Church's one foundation
350 We will walk through the valley
386 Again the Lord's own day (E/G)
Your choice....

501 I am the bread of life
525 Jesus, you are Lord
526 Keep in mind
670 One thing I ask (Ps 26/27) (Comm/CT)
746 God is my great desire
781 Centre of my life
AK16

Sunday 33 *Your endurance will win you your lives*

Malachi 3:19–20; Ps 97(98); 2 Thess 3:7–12; LUKE 21:5–19

28 At the name of Jesus	724 All the ends of the earth (cf Resp Ps) (E/G)
45 Colours of day	739 Father we come to you (E/G)
165 Lead us, heavenly Father	752 Gather us in (E/G)
221 O God of earth and altar (E/G)	772 New songs of celebration (cf Resp Ps)
331 Thy hand, O God, has guided (CT/R)	792 Sing a new song (cf Resp Ps) (E/G)
405 Awake, awake! (E/G)	793 Sing all creation (E/G)
480 God is working his purpose out	800 The voice of God (CT/R)
498 Hills of the north, rejoice	806 Wake your power (CT/R)
613 The King shall come	810 We have a king
640 Wake up! the dawn is near	AK29 (cf Resp Ps)
644 We gather together (E/G)	

Your choice....

Sunday 34 *I rejoiced when I heard them say:*
Let us go to God's house

2 Sam 5:1–3; Ps 121(122); Col 1:11–20; LUKE 23:35–43

56 Crown him with many crowns	470 Give praise to the Lord (E/G)
78 Forth in thy name, O Lord (CT/R)	493 He is Lord
107 Hail redeemer, King divine	506 I met you at the cross
121 Holy God, we praise thy name (E/G)	605 Sing to the world (CT/R)
151 Jesu, meek and lowly	687 Ps 121(122) (Resp Ps)
206 My song is love unknown	715 Christus vincit (CT/R)
318 The royal banners forward go	795 Sing it in the valleys = AK84 (CT/R)
324 They say I am wise	804 To Jesus Christ our sovereign King (CT/R)
332 To Christ the Lord of worlds	755 I rejoiced (cf Resp Ps)
429 Christ is the world's redeemer (see Tunefinder)	AK35 (cf Resp Ps), 84

Your choice....

Feast Days
and Days of Special Prayer

December 8   The Immaculate Conception of the Blessed Virgin Mary
Before the world began, God chose us in Christ
Genesis 3:9–15,20; Ps 97(98); Eph 1:3–6,11–12; LUKE 1:26–38

109	Hail thou star of ocean	572	Of one that is so fair
126	Holy Virgin, by God's decree	609	Tell out, my soul
192	Mary Immaculate, star of the morning	611	The angel Gabriel (cf Gosp)
290	Star of ocean lead us	724	All the ends of the earth (cf Resp Ps)
365	Ye who own the faith of Jesus	792	Sing a new song (cf Resp Ps)
381	A noble flower of Juda	816	What do you want of me, Lord?
382	A sign is seen in heaven		AK74
479	God has gladdened my heart		

Your choice....

February 2   The Presentation of the Lord
A light to enlighten the Gentiles
Malachi 3:1–4; Ps 23(24); Hebrews 2:14–18; LUKE 2:22–40 (or 22–32)

46	Come, adore this wondrous presence (comm)	552	Lumen Christi!
110	Hail to the Lord's anointed	561	Now let your people (Nunc Dimittis)
166	Let all mortal flesh	614	The light of Christ
188	Maiden, yet a mother	695	At last, all-powerful Master (Nunc Dimittis)
242	Open your ears	668	Psalm 23(24) (Resp.Ps)
281	Sing of Mary	733	Come to set us free
286	Songs of thankfulness and praise	768	Shine, Jesus, shine
315	The race that long in darkness		AK14 (cf Resp Ps)
428	Christ is the world's light		

Your choice....

June 24   The Birth of St John the Baptist
What will this child turn out to be?
Vigil readings: Jer 1:4–10; Ps 70(71); I Pet 1:8–12; LUKE 1:5–17
Day mass readings: Is 49:1–6; Ps 138(139); Acts 13:22–26; LUKE 1:57–66,80
General Saints hymns, also:

16	A voice cries in the wilderness = AK71	693	The Benedictus
385	Across the years	744	Forth in the peace of Christ
557	My God, you fathom my heart (cf Resp Ps)	789	Prepare ye the way
574	Oh the word of my Lord	819	When John baptised
638	Yahweh I know you are near (cf Resp Ps)		AK71

Your choice....

97

June 29 Saints Peter and Paul
I have fought the good fight to the end
Vigil readings: Acts 3:1–10; Ps 18(19); Gal 1:11–20; JOHN 21:15–19
Day mass readings: Acts 12:1–11; Ps 33(34); 2 Tim 4:6–8,17–18; MATTHEW 16:13–19
General Saints hymns, also:

60	Dear Lord and Father of mankind	515	If God is for us
73	Fight the good fight (2R)	550	Lord, you have come to the lakeside
331	Thy hand, O God, has guided	773	Nothing can ever take away from us
445	Do you really love me	AK17	(cf Resp Ps)
458	Feed my lambs, my son		

Your choice....

August 6 The Transfiguration of the Lord
They saw his glory
Daniel 7:9–10,13–14; Ps 96(97); 2 Peter 1:16–19; Year A: MATTHEW 17:1–9; Year B:MARK
9:2–10; Year C: Luke 9:28–36

35	Be thou my vision	428	Christ is the world's light
36	Blest are the pure in heart	570	O raise your eyes on high
42	Christ is King of earth and heaven	667	Psalm 26(27)
46	Come, adore this wondrous presence	727	Before the heaven and earth
95	Godhead here in hiding	737	Eye has not seen
123	Holy, holy, holy	739	Father, we come to you
134	Immortal, invisible	748	God, your glory we have seen
203	My God, how wonderful thou art	768	Shine, Jesus, shine
270	Rejoice! the Lord is king	815	We walk by faith

Your choice....

August 15 The Assumption of the Blessed Virgin Mary
The Almighty has done great things for me:
*   he has exalted the lowly*
Vigil readings: I Chron 15:3–4,15–16; 16:1–2; Ps 131(132); I Cor 15:54–57; LUKE 11:27–28.
Day mass readings: Apoc 11:19; 12:1–6.10; Ps 44(45); I Cor 15:20–27; LUKE 1:39–56

106	Hail Queen of heaven	365	Ye who own the faith of Jesus
132	I'll sing a hymn to Mary	382	A sign is seen in heaven (2R)
142	I sing the Lord God's praises	527	Of one who is so fair
188	Maiden yet a mother	609	Tell out, my soul
281	Sing of Mary	694	The Magnificat
290	Star of ocean	749	Great is the Lord

Your choice....

September 14   The Triumph of the Cross
The Son of Man must be lifted up
Numbers 21:4–9; Ps 77(78); Phil 2:6–11; JOHN 3:13–17

42 Christ is King of earth and heaven	486 Good Christian men
179 Lord Jesus Christ	493 He is Lord
279 Sing, my tongue, the glorious battle	506 I met you at the cross
318 The royal banners	522 Jesus, the holy Lamb of God (2R)
355 When I survey	526 Keep in mind
419 By the cross	575 On a hill far away
428 Christ is the world's light	605 Sing to the world of Christ (CT/R)
429 Christ is the world's redeemer (see Tunefinder)	737 Before the heaven and earth (2R)

Your choice....

October 25   The English Martyrs
You will show me the path of life
Heb 11:33–40; Ps 15(16); JOHN 12:24–26 or JOHN 15:18–21
General Saints hymns, also:

68 Faith of our fathers	463 For to those who love God
77 For all the saints	489 Greater love has no man
331 Thy hand, O God	646 We praise you, Lord
429 Christ is the world's Redeemer (see Tunefinder)	696 The Beatitudes
	773 Nothing can ever take away
444 Do not be afraid	781 Centre of my life (cf Resp Ps)
449 Father, hear the prayer	812 Unless a grain of wheat (Comm/CT)

Your choice....

November 1   All Saints
Theirs is the kingdom of heaven
Apoc 7:2–4,9–14; Ps 23(24); I John 3:1–3; MATTHEW 5:1–12
General Saints hymns, also:

265 Praise we now the Lord our God	387 Alabare (1R)
266 Praise we our God with joy	699 The Beatitudes (Gosp)
320 The Kingdom (Gosp) = AK73	726 As a tree planted (Gosp)
331 Thy hand, O God	

Your choice....

November 2   All Souls
I Hope in him, hold firm and take heart
Various texts. Isaiah 25:6–9; Choice of Psalms includes 22(23) and 26(27); Romans 5:5–11; Gosp
A: MATTHEW 11:25–30; B: MARK 15:33–39; 16:1–6; C: LUKE 7:11–17

81 From the deep	222 O God, our help in ages past
115 Help, Lord, the souls	267 Promised Lord and Christ is he
149 Jerusalem the golden	300 The Church's one foundation

302 The day of resurrection
569 O light forever dawning
667 Ps 22(23)
670 Ps 26(27)
674 Ps 62(63)
Your choice....

675 Ps 83(84)
737 Eye has not seen
763 Jesus, lead the way
779 O how lovely is your dwelling place
791 Safe in the shadow

November 9 The Dedication of St John Lateran
You are God's temple
Ezekiel 47:1–2,8–9,12; Ps 45(46); I Cor 3:9–11,16–17; JOHN 2:13–22

121 Holy God, we praise thy name
139 Into one we all are gathered
168 Let all the world in every corner
184 Love divine, all loves excelling
240 On this house your blessing, Lord
264 Praise to the Lord, the Almighty (PG)
265 Praise we now the Lord our God (CT/R)
300 The Church's one foundation
344 We celebrate this festive day (E/G)
358 Where is love and lovingkindness
399 An upper room
Your choice....

427 Christ is made the sure foundation
472 Glorious things of thee are spoken (E/G)
612 The Church is wherever
643 We form one Church
675 Ps 83(84) My soul is longing
687 Ps 121(122) I rejoiced
752 Gather us in (E/G)
755 I rejoiced
779 Oh how lovely is your dwelling place
818 What is this place (E/G)
AK16, 35

OTHER SAINTS' DAYS

St David   s4 O great St David

St Patrick 105 Hail glorious St Patrick
                645 We praise you and thank you

St Joseph   s6 Hail, holy Joseph

St George 163 Leader now on earth no longer

St Andrew 103 Great St Andrew
                s5 St Andrew, called to follow Christ

General Saints' Hymns

35 Be thou my vision
36 Blest are the pure in heart
60 Dear Lord and Father of mankind
77 For all the saints
119 He who would valiant be
149 Jerusalem the golden
320 The Kingdom
331 Thy hand, O God, has guided
380 A new commandment
387 Alabare
394 Alleluia! sons of God
429 Christ is the world's redeemer

444 Do not be afraid
449 Father, hear the prayer
460 Follow me, follow me
463 For to those who love God
508 Here I am, Lord
515 If God is for us (esp. Martyrs)
550 Lord, you have come to the lakeside
646 We praise you, Lord (Te Deum)
656 Who wants to live as God
699 The Beatitudes
719 Te Deum laudamus
726 As a tree planted
743 Come we that love the Lord
AK73, 86

For the Anniversary of the Dedication of a Church
See November 9, St John Lateran

100

Days of Special Prayer

Mass for Justice and Peace

(Celebrated on the 4th Sunday in Ordinary Time)

25 Attend and keep this happy fast (see Tunefinder)
72 Feed us now
142 I sing the Lord God's praises
189 Make me a channel
190 Man of Galilee
314 The prophet in his hunger
317 There is a world
320 The Kingdom
352 Whatsoever you do
376 A certain traveller
397 Almighty Father, who for us
417 But I say unto you
436 Come, Lord Jesus
462 For the healing of the nations
479 God has gladdened my heart
488 Grant us thy peace
532 Let all who share one bread
553 May the peace of the Lord
554 Modern man has the city
581 Peace is my parting gift
591 Return to the Lord

593 Seek first the kingdom
608 Tell out, my soul
628 This is what Yahweh asks
636 Unite us, Lord, in peace
644 We gather together
726 As a tree planted
729 Christ's church shall glory
743 Forgive our sins as we forgive
744 Forth in the peace of Christ
749 Great is the Lord
767 Lead us from death to life
797 The gift of the Holy Spirit
798 The kingdom of God
799 The Master came to bring good news
800 The voice of God
817 What does the Lord require?

Responsorial Psalms:
676 Ps 84(84)
687 Ps 121(122)

AK24, 25, 35, 39

Mass for the Unity of Christians

There is no such thing as a definitive list of hymns for this or other ecumenical occasions. The act of worshipping together is a gesture of unity and many other hymns and songs could be chosen which do not have 'unity' as their explicit theme.

Healing divisions

331 Thy hand, O God, has guided
342 We are one in the Spirit
380 A new commandment
443 Divided our pathways
629 Thou whose almighty word
783 O that today
799 The master came
AK77

Christ draws us together (e.g. in Baptism*)

136 In Christ there is no East or West
300 The Church's one foundation
327 This is my will
409 Bind us together
427 Christ is made the sure foundation
472 Glorious things of you are spoken
*621 There is one Lord
622 Thine be the glory
729 Christ's Church shall glory
*826 You have put on Christ
AK81, 83

Eucharist, Sacrament of Unity

249 O thou who at thy Eucharist
399 An upper room
501 I am the bread of life

Unity in Mission

76 Follow Christ
468 Gathered here (see Tunefinder)
605 Sing to the world
612 The Church is wherever
632 To be the body of the Lord
644 We gather together
744 Forth in the peace of Christ
753 How shall they hear
797 The gift of the Holy Spirit
798 The Kingdom of God
807 We are your people
809 We have a Gospel to proclaim

Psalms

667 Psalm 22(23)   AK13, 30, 35
680 Psalm 99(100)
687 Ps 121(122)
(see also hymn paraphrases of these Psalms)

Mass for God's Blessing on Human Work

51	Come, Lord Jesus, come	296	Take my hands
63	Do not worry	411	Blest are you
79	Forth in thy name, O Lord	469	Gifts of bread and wine
135	In bread we bring you	483	God our maker, mighty Father
138	In the earth	547	Lord of creation
181	Lord of all hopefulness	608	Take my life
190	Man of Galilee	637	Upon thy table
211	Now thank we all our God	821	With open hands

Mass in Thanksgiving for the Harvest

4	All creatures of our God and King	402	As long as men on earth
14	All this world belongs to Jesus	410	Blest are you, Lord God
55	Come, ye thankful people	461	For the fruits of his creation
138	In the earth		
211	Now thank we all our God	478	God gives us harvest
218	O Father, take in sign of love	615	The Lord is my shepherd
268	Reap me the earth	821	With open hands
307	The green life rises		Responsorial Psalms:
346	We plough the fields	688	Ps 125(126)

Mass for the Spread of the Gospel (Mission Sunday)

45	Colours of day	661	You must cry out the Word
78/744	Forth in the peace of Christ	703	Go out to the whole world (round)
99	Go tell everyone	724	All the ends of the earth
102	God's Spirit is in my heart	744	see 78
313	The Mass is ended	753	How shall they hear the word
331	Thy hand, O God, has guided	758	In the land there is a hunger
395	Alleluia, give thanks to the risen Lord	788	Praise to you, O Christ
480	God is working his purpose out	797	The gift of the Holy Spirit
500	Our God reigns	809	We have a Gospel
550	Lord, you have come to the lakeside		
574	Oh the word of my Lord		Responsorial Psalms:
619	The Spirit of God rests upon me	685	Psalm 116(117)
629	Thou whose almighty Word		AK29

Hymns for the Sacraments and Other Rites

Christian Initiation

See page 21 for a general introduction to this section. (Numbers in brackets refer to paragraphs in the text of RCIA)

1. Rite of Acceptance into the Order of Catechumens

This takes place at a time to be decided by each community.

Gathering (48):
325 This day God gives me
508 Here I am, Lord
659 Yahweh, I know you are near
728 Bless the Lord, my soul
779 Oh how lovely is your dwelling place
794 Sing of the Lord's goodness

Greeting (49):
674 Psalm 62
746 God is my great desire
778 Oh God, I seek you
812 Unless a grain of wheat
AK22, 34

Signing (54):
444 Do not be afraid
557 My God, you fathom my heart
777 O Christe Domine Jesu
AK76

Intercessions
710 O Lord, hear my prayer

Closing Song
706/707 Jubilate Deo
749 Great is the Lord
AK86

2. The Rite of Election
This takes place on the 1st Sunday of Lent

Gathering
793 Sing all creation
752 Gather us in

Enrollment
550 Lord, you have come to the lakeside
781 Centre of my life

Psalms
18(19), 22(23), 23(24), 41(42), 62(63)
AK13, 22

Gospel Acc.
788 Praise to you, O Christ

After the Witness:
473 Glory and praise to our God
508 I the Lord of sea and sky

Signing of Names (132):
444 Do not be afraid
659 Yahweh, I know you are near

Closing song
815 We walk by faith

3. The Scrutinies
See Sundays 3, 4 and 5 of Lent, Year A, pp.000–000

4. The Celebration of Initiation
(See also The Easter Vigil, p.39).

Thirsting for God
671 Ps 41(42)
674 Ps 62(63)
728 Bless the Lord, my soul
746 God is my great desire
778 Oh God, I seek you

Faith
75 Firmly I believe and truly
130 I believe in God the Father

Acclamations and Refrains
430 Christ our Lord has come to save
559 New life
621 There is one Lord

784 Oh healing river
812 Unless a grain of wheat
826 You have put on Christ
     Water of Life
AK1

Psalms
667 Ps 22(23)
670 Ps 26(27)
673 Ps 50(51)
688 Psalm 125(126)
756 If God should lead us (Ps 125/126)
AK22, 34, 35

Prayer and Trust
383 Abba, Father
475 God at creation's dawn
659 Yahweh, I know you are near
700 Breath of life
710 O Lord, hear my prayer

Giving thanks
244 O praise ye the Lord
260 Praise, my soul, the King of heaven
384 Abba, Father, send your Spirit
394 Alleluia, sons of God, arise
405 Awake, awake
420 Called to be servants
456 Fear not, rejoice and be glad
463 For to those who love God
477 God forgave my sin
479 God has gladdened my heart
580 Out of deep unordered water
609 Tell out, my soul
614 The light of Christ
620 There is a river
779 Oh how lovely is your dwelling place
794 Sing of the Lord's goodness

Mission
  78/744 Forth in the peace of Christ
444 Do not be afraid
508 Here I am, Lord

Infant Baptism
116 Here's a child for you
154 Jesus, gentlest Saviour
292 Suffer little children
312 The Lord's my shepherd
384 Abba, Father, send your Spirit
667 Psalm 22(23)
670 Psalm 26(27)

5. Confirmation
37 Breathe on me, breath of God
49 Come down, O love divine
50 Come, Holy Ghost, Creator, come
51 Come, Lord Jesus, come
78/744 Forth in the peace of Christ
93 God be in my head
99 God's Spirit is in my heart
289 Spirit of the living God
383/4 Abba, Father
460 Follow me
502 I am the vine
510 I will be with you
545 Lord, in everything I do
547 Lord of creation
574 Oh the word of my Lord
594–6 Send forth your Spirit
608 Take my life
617 The Spirit is moving
619 The Spirit of God
638 Veni Sancte Spiritus
657 Wind and fire
663 You shall cross the barren desert
700 Breath of life
744 see 78
781 Centre of my life
797 The gift of the Holy Spirit
806 Wake your power
809 We have a gospel to proclaim
811 We have been told
816 What do you want of me, Lord?
823 You shall go out with joy

Psalms

667 Psalm 22(23)
682 Psalm 103(104)
685 Psalm 116(117)
691 Psalm 144(145)

Reception of a baptized person into full communion with the Catholic Church
Choose from the Baptism and Confirmation sections. The following psalms are especially suitable:

670 Psalm 26(27)
671 Psalm 41(42)
674 Psalm 62(63)
504/5 Psalm 120(121)
AK34, 66

Worship of the Eucharist outside Mass

Adoration

95 Godhead here in hiding
157 Jesus, my Lord, my God, my All
213 O bread of heaven
220 O Godhead hid
294 Sweet Sacrament divine
696 Adoramus te, Domine
754 I received the living God
764 Jesus, Lord of life and love
777 O Christe Domine Jesu

Banquet

7 Alleluia! sing to Jesus
27 At the Lamb's high feast
774 Now in this banquet
802 Behold the Lamb of God

Bread of Life

412 Bread of the world
521 Jesus said: I am the bread
523 Jesus the Lord said

Food

166 Let all mortal flesh
438 Come, O Lord
567 O food of travellers
597 Shepherd of souls

Last Supper

185 Love is his word
399 An upper room

408 Before Christ died
501 I am the bread of life
623 This is my body
653 When the time came
812 Unless a grain of wheat

Sacrament of Unity

136 In Christ there is no east or west
139 Into one we all are gathered
249 O thou who at thy Eucharist
403 As one body

Praise

543 Lord, enthroned in heavenly splendour
605 Sing to the world of Christ
788 Praise now your God
794 Sing of the Lord's goodness

Hymns for the Rite
Verbum supernum/O Salutaris:

245 O salutaris (English)
372 O salutaris (Latin)
373 O salutaris (English, another version)
309 Complete in English

Pange Lingua/Tantum Ergo:

219 Complete in English
716 Complete in Latin
374 Tantum Ergo (Latin)
375 Tantum Ergo (English)

Penance and Reconciliation

Sorrow

81 From the deep I lift my voice
98 God of mercy and compassion
144 It's me, O Lord
165 Lead us, heavenly Father
180 Lord Jesus, think on me
191 Many times I have turned
221 O God of earth and altar
223 O God, thy people gather
247 O sacred head sore wounded

330 Thou wilt keep him in perfect peace
338 Vaster far than any ocean
385 Across the years
397 Almighty Father, who for us
400 As earth that is dry
443 Divided our pathways
454 Father of heaven, whose love profound
542 Lord, confronted with your might
544 Lord, graciously hear us
577 Our Father, we have wandered

591 Return to the Lord
660 You, Israel, return now
673 Ps 50(51) Have mercy on me, God
689 Ps 129(130) Out of the depths
711 Ostende nobis
751 Hear us, almighty Lord
757 In the abundance of your compassion
770 My people, I hear you calling
771 My soul cannot be still
780 O Lord, be not mindful

How God wants us to live

417 But I say unto you
743 Forgive our sins as we forgive
797 The gift of the Holy Spirit
799 The Master came to bring good news

807 We are your people
817 What does the Lord require

Forgiveness
60 Dear Lord and Father
227 O Lord my God
231 O the love of my Lord
260 Praise, my soul, the King of heaven
266 Praise we our God with joy
273 Seasons come, seasons go
340 Walk with me, O my Lord
350 We will walk
477 God forgave my sin
728 Bless the Lord, my soul
750 Who calls my life again
773 Nothing can ever take away
803 To God be the glory
813 We're forgiven

Marriage

See page 23 for a general introduction to this section.

 71 Father, within thy house today
139 Into one we all are gathered
165 Lead us, heavenly Father
184 Love divine, all loves excelling
243 O perfect love
280 Sing of the bride
311 The King of love
312 The Lord's my shepherd
320 The Kingdom (The Beatitudes) = AK71
327 This is my will, my one command
358 Where are love and loving-kindness
380 A new commandment
404 As the bridegroom to his chosen
450 Father I place into your hands
699 The Beatitudes
738 Father, we come in prayer = AK78
741 For the beauty
AK78, 83

Psalms

667 Psalm 22(23)
681 Psalm 102(103)

Anniversary

Other suitable hymns may be found under *Thanksgiving*.
211 Now thank we all our God
260 Praise, my soul
609 Tell out, my soul
681 Psalm 102(103)
691 Psalm 144(145)
728 Bless the Lord, my soul
741 For the beauty of the earth

Ordination, Religious Profession

s7 Lord, make me an instrument
35 Be thou my vision
50 Come, Holy Ghost
51 Come, Lord Jesus, come
73 Fight the good fight
78/744 Forth in the peace of Christ
99 God's Spirit is in my heart
111 Happy the man
119 He who would valiant be
189 Make me a channel
201 My God, accept my heart
319 The Spirit of the Lord
327 This is my will
389 All my hope on God is founded
399 An upper room
404 As the bridegroom to his chosen
445 Do you really love me?
449 Father, hear the prayer we offer
460 Follow me
500 How lovely on the mountains
508 Here I am, Lord
530 Leave your country
545 Lord, in everything I do

547 Lord of creation
550 Lord, you have come to the lakeside
574 Oh the word of my Lord
608 Take my life
638 Veni sancte Spiritus
703 Go out to the whole world
707 Jubilate Deo
720 Veni creator Spiritus
726 As a tree planted
744 see 78
753 How shall they hear the word
779 Oh how lovely is your dwelling place
781 Centre of my life
797 The gift of the Holy Spirit
809 We have a gospel to proclaim
816 What do you want of me, Lord?

Psalms

670 Psalm 26(27)
674 Psalm 62(63)
675 Psalm 84(84)
680 Psalm 99(100)

Anointing of the Sick

1 Abide with me
15 All ye who seek a comfort sure
23 Ask and you shall receive
32/3 Be still and know
97 God is love: his the care
150 Jesu, lover of my soul
164 Lead, kindly light
181 Lord of all hopefulness
208 Now come to me
289 Spirit of the living God
312 The Lord's my shepherd
362 Yahweh, you are my strength
389 All my hope on God is founded
406 Bartimaeus
407 Be still, my soul
415 Bright star of morning
444 Do not be afraid
450 Father, I place into your hands
540/5 I lift up my eyes (=AK)
517 In God alone is there rest for my soul
528 Lay your hands
538 Like the deer that thirsts
558 My soul is longing
579 Our Saviour Jesus Christ proclaimed

581 Peace is my parting gift
635 Trust in the Lord
742 For you, O Lord
746 God is my great desire
763 Jesus, lead the way
773 Nothing can ever take away
775 O changeless Christ
776 O Christ the healer
777 O Christe Domine Jesu (several psalms)
778 O God, I seek you (cf Ps 62)
779 Oh how lovely is your dwelling
791 Safe in the shadow
808 We give God thanks

667 Psalm 22(23)
670 Psalm 26(27)
671 Psalm 41(42)
674 Psalm 62(63)
675 Psalm 84(84)
681 Psalm 102(103)
687 Psalm 121(122)
689 Psalm 129(130)
AK 10, 21, 22, 27, 34, 36

The Rite of Funerals

See page 23 for a general introduction to this section.

Reception of the Body

670 Psalm 26(27)
671 Psalm 41(42)
687 Psalm 121(122)
763 Jesus, lead the way
777 O Christe Domine Jesu

Mass
Entrance/Gathering

696 Adoramus te, Domine
711 Ostende nobis, Domine
742 For you, O Lord
746 God is my great desire
777 O Christe, Domine Jesu
779 Oh how lovely

Liturgy of the Word

667 Psalm 22(23)
(also no 777, or hymn versions)
669 Psalm 24(25)
670 Psalm 26(27)
671 Psalm 41(42) (also no 538)
674 Psalm 62(63) (also no 778)
681 Psalm 102(103) (also no 728)
687 Psalm 121(122)
689 Psalm 129(130) (also no 777)
AK13, 16, 26, 27, 36

Gospel Acclamations

788 Praise to you (Lent)

Intercessions:

710 O Lord, hear my prayer
Divine Office section intercessions

Liturgy of the Eucharist
Preparation of Gifts:
Instrumental or choral music, or a
period of quiet

Communion

Lamb of God 2–4, Eucharist section
777 O Christe Domine Jesu
812 Unless a grain of wheat

Other hymn suggestions

149 Jerusalem the golden
164 Lead, kindly light
181 Lord of all hopefulness
208 Now come to me (see Tunefinder)
222 O God our help in ages past
311 The king of love
312 The Lord's my shepherd
350 We will walk through the valley
501 I am the bread of life
517 In God alone
526 Keep in mind
569 O light forever dawning

Song of farewell

 77 For all the saints
763 Jesus, lead the way
812 Unless a grain of wheat

The Funeral of a child

181 Lord of all hopefulness
292 Suffer little children
311 The king of love
312 The Lord's my shepherd
444 Do not be afraid
670 Psalm 26(27)
773 Nothing can ever take away

Psalms

667 Psalm 22(23)
(also no 777, or hymn versions)
669 Psalm 24(25)
671 Psalm 41(42) (also no 538)

Tunefinder

Use this section to find alternative tunes to words which otherwise risk being ignored because 'we don't know the tune'. If you don't like the suggestion given, you will find more in the Metrical Index – or in other hmnbooks. Some of the tunes suggested here are in fact not in the Celebration Hymnal and these are italicised.

25 Attend and keep this happy fast (8686D)	Ellacombe, 'Bach' (344), *Kingsfold*
46 Come adore this wondrous presence (878787)	Mannheim
142 I sing the Lord God's Praises (7676D)	Cruger, King's Lynn
186 Loving Father, from thy bounty (878787)	Oriel
208 Now come to me all you who seek (8686D)	Ellacombe, *Kingsfold*
217 O Father, now the hour has come (8686)	St Bernard
223 O God, thy people gather (7676D)	King's Lynn, *Wolvercote*
224 O God, we give ourselves today (8686)	Ballerma
272 Round me falls the night	Seelenbräutigam
275 See us, Lord, about thine altar (8787)	*Drakes Boughton*
408 Before Christ died (8686)	St Magnus, Belmont
422 Christ be my way	*Londonderry Air*
429 Christ is the world's redeemer (7676D)	King's Lynn, Aurelia
446 Each morning with its new-born light (8888)	*Wareham*, Rockingham, Tallis' Canon, *Vom Himmel Hoch*
459 Firm is our faith (8888)	Duke Street, Fulda
461 For the fruits of his creation	Ar Hyd y Nos (All through the Night)
462 For the healing of the nations (878787)	Westminster Abbey, *Neander*
468 Gathered here from many churches (878788)	*All Saints*
483 God our maker, mighty Father (8787D)	Abbot's Leigh, Westminster Abbey
497 Help us accept each other (7676D)	Willsbridge
546 Lord Jesus Christ, be present now (8888)	Breslau
564 Now with the fading light of day (8888)	Gonfalon Royal, O Waly waly
580 Out of deep unordered water (8787D)	*Blaenwern*
612 The church is wherever (12.10.12.11)	Kremser (with some adjustment)
633 To God our Father be the praise (8686)	Richmond, *Abridge*
651 When Jesus comes to be baptized (8888)	Stuttgart, Westminster New
747 God who spoke in the beginning (878787)	Mannheim

ITALICISED TUNES will be found in one or other of the following books: *Praise the Lord* (1972), *Parish Hymn Book*, *Hymns Ancient and Modern* and *Hymns for Today's Church*.

Songs for Choirs and Singing Groups
Hints for Singing

N.B. All of these are capable of use as congregation pieces as well. Singing them as motets may be a preliminary stage in teaching them to the congregation; or a variation on the usual method of performance.

Water of Life (Eucharist) See OCP/Thomas More Octavo version, no 7125
Eucharistic Liturgy I (Farrell) See OCP/Thomas More Octavo version, no 7130
Eucharistic Liturgy IV (Inwood) See OCP/Thomas More Octavo version, no 7117

397	Choir piece for Preparation of Gifts	652	ditto, even if a bit Victorian
402	Choir piece for Preparation of Gifts	656	see 505
404	Choir piece for Communion	670	See OCP/Thomas More Octavo version, no 7157
406	Choir piece for Prep of Gifts, Sunday 30/B	696	Extra instrumental parts in Music from Taizé II, (Instr)
412	Choir motet: Communion	706	ditto
418	Use refrain as an ostinato, Taizé style	707	ditto: also nos 709–11, 728
423	Motet for Easter Sunday/Eastertide	724	Harmony provided in the verses
437	Choir carol for Advent or Christmas	726	Ditto. Look at the rest of *Mass of Creation*, (GIA)
454	Motet for Lent	734	An oustanding new tune, rather difficult for congregation
461	For the harvest season	737	Work on the harmony in the verses
470	If too difficult for people to learn in full, just teach the Alleluias	739	See OCP/Thomas More Octavo version, no 7153
488	Motet with obvious applications	740	see 734
505	A fine piece but needs practice, which is usual with music by Huijbers	747	ditto, but see Tunefinder
531	ditto. Contrast voices between verse (solo or semichorus) and refrain	750	Plainchant – modern ears are unused to it but they shouldn't be
545	The beautiful choir arrangement of verse 2 is well worth the effort	756	see 505
		777	Extra instrumental parts in Music from Taizé II, Instrumental
563	For Advent	778	see 737
566	For Advent	779	ditto
569	For funerals/Remembrance Sunday	782	ditto
572	Our Lady; Advent Sunday 4. Alternate ladies/men (Latin/English)	787	ditto
582	More effective for choir because variation (harmony/unison; ladies/men) can be introduced into verses	789	See OCP/Thomas More Octavo version, no 7195
		790	see Music from Taizé II
591	A good song but rather high for congregations; worth transposing to D min	806	See 505
		812	See OCP/Thomas More Octavo version, no 7115
597	Could be harmony or unison.	814	See OCP/Thomas More Octavo version, no 7160
605	See OCP/Thomas More Octavo version, no 7113		
615	An unusual version of this psalm	815	see 726
616	A solo piece?	817	see 734
633	Can be sung to another tune, but this one is worth hearing too	822	see 737
640	Good words and tune: rather have the choir sing it than no-one		

COMPLETE ALPHABETICAL INDEX OF TUNES

METRICAL INDEX

87.87.87

St Thomas 46, 177, 219, 279, 372/3
Kensington 747
Mannheim 165
Picardy 166, 186
Praise my soul 260
Oriel 335
Regent Square 543

88.88.88

Surrey 71
St Catherine 213
Sunset 295

65.65D

Laudes 109
Une vraie crainte 188

66.86D Double Short Metre, DSM
Corona 56 (i)
Diademata 56 (ii)

76.76D

Aurelia 233, 300, 516

Ave Virgo Virginum 433, 820
Baronita 497
Cruger 110
Ellacombe 302
Ewing 149
Kings Lynn 221 (i)
Magnificat 142
Moville 429
Neshanic 577 (ii)
O King of might 234
Passion Chorale 247, 569, 577 (i)
Picardy 166, 186, 462
Royal Oak 13
St Theodulph 8
Thornbury 332
Turris Davidica 132
Vaughan 176
Westminster Abbey 427
Willsbridge 221 (ii)

77.77D

Salzburg 27
Westminster Old 40
St George 55
King divine 107
Aberystwyth 150
St Edmund 286
Charlton 545

86.86D Double Common Metre, DCM

Claudius 25
Ellacombe, modified 156
Come to me 208
Forest Green 235
Festive day 344

87.87D

Abbot's Leigh 453, 472
Austria 585
Hyfrydol 7
Daily, daily 57 (i)
Laudes Mariae 57 (ii)
Au sang qu'un Dieu 98
Contemplation 103
Swavesey 163
Pleading Saviour 281
Rex Gloriae 483

98.98D

Rendez á Dieu 772, 819

HYMNS BASED ON SCRIPTURE

GENESIS
12:1ff 530

I KINGS
17:11–16 314

ISAIAH
9:2–7 315
9:6 436, 464
12:2–6 814
35:5–6.10 664
40:28–31 635
40:1–2,4,9 566
40:3.5 805 vv.2–4
40:3–4.9–11 16
40:31–32 630
43:1–2 663

43:1–4 444
43:2,4,10,18–20 456
45:8 587, 732
49:15 630
49:15–16a 511
52:7–10 500
54:6–10 630
55:1–2 779
55:1–2,6,9,12 400
55:1.10–12 Water of Life
58:5–9 25
58:7 591 (v2)
61:1–2 319, 496 (v.3), 619)

JEREMIAH
1:4–10 574
4:19.23–25; 17:12–13 771

31:2.3.8 etc. 770
31:31 591

DANIEL
3:52ff 3, 12, 796

HOSEA
6:4 591

JOEL
2:13 Water of Life (v.4)
2:21–23,27; 3:2; 4:18 457
3:1ff 617

MICAH
6:8 628
6:6–8 817

INDEX OF PSALM VERSIONS

Some psalms have two numbers. This is because of a discrepancy between the numbering in the Hebrew version of the bible (used by Jews and the reformed churches) and the Greek version (used until now by the Catholic church.) This means for example that what in the Authorised Version is known as the Twenty-Third Psalm (The Lord's my shepherd) is Psalm 22 in Catholic liturgical books; and likewise the psalm with the tune known as The Old Hundredth is Psalm 99. Both numberings are given here but it is likely that the Hebrew numbering will eventually displace the Greek.

116

TOPICAL INDEX